M000195775

Ten Reasons Why You Must Not Give Up

Samuel Kee

Foreword by Keith Robinson,
Founder of Emerge, Inc.

Ellechor Publishing House, LLC
2431 NW Wessex Terr, Hillsboro, OR 97124

Copyright © 2010 by Samuel Kee
2011 Ellechor Publishing House Paperback Edition
Kee, Samuel, 1976-
Hope Stands/ Samuel Kee.
ISBN: 978-0-9826242-7-2
Library of Congress Control Number: 2011935413

Ellechor Publishing House,
2431 NW Wessex Terr,
Hillsboro, OR 97124

Printed in the United States of America

www.ellechorpublishing.com

Praise for Hope Stands

"*Hope Stands* is a book for the hopeless and for those who love them. Sam Kee reaches out and touches those who struggle with life and gives them reasons for living. I enthusiastically recommend this book."

Tremper Longman
Co-Author of Cry of the Soul
Robert H. Gundry, Professor of Biblical Studies at Westmont College

"Sam Kee is a gifted writer with a compelling message. He will grab your attention on the first page and pull you towards light and hope in Jesus Christ. If you are battling with despair—or know someone who is—read this book."

Colin Smith
Author of the Unlocking the Bible series
Senior Pastor at The Orchard in Arlington Heights, IL

"Sam Kee's book offers Hope to those who for any reason find themselves thinking "I can't take this anymore...there's only one solution...one thing to make it all stop." But Sam points to others in the Scriptures and outside of them who discovered that the darkness projected a reflected light that only it could make visible..."

Mike Kellogg
Senior Announcer with Moody Radio
Host of Music Thru The Night

"There is a movement of God happening in northern Chicagoland, and Sam Kee is in the middle of it! He has helped mobilize youth leaders and students as they declare their dependence on God and their desire to link arms around a mission. Sam listens to students. Sam listens to parents. Sam listens to youth pastors. This book flows out of that listening and does battle against a dark enemy attacking our youth. It is a must read for anyone that wants to help declare and demonstrate that hope stands!"

Bill Yaccino
Executive Director
Christ Together, Chicago

"Sam Kee, a veteran youth pastor, has lots of first-hand experience with the deep sense of hopelessness that threatens to define (or destroy) the lives of some of the teens with whom he works. He realizes that hopelessness is not limited to a single demographic. To that end, Kee realizes that the only antidote for hopelessness is anchored in the resurrection of Jesus Christ. He's identified ten reasons why hope exists in each one of our lives, using the Biblical account of the resurrection as both guide and promise. He wants his readers to see hope. He wants his readers to hear the resurrected Christ proclaiming life!

Hope Stands is an accessible guide to the hope that is rooted in Jesus Christ. It is an easy read with an important message that has the potential to change the course of a despairing person's life."

Michelle Van Loon
Author of Parable Life

4

"Sam Kee is a cheerleader in the game called life, urging us all to get up out of hopelessness or fear and win this game because Jesus is on our side.

All of the cheers are actually strong theology drawn from the scenes around our Lord's empty tomb, from which He stood up so victoriously.

Very compelling and motivating!"

Knute Larson
Evangelical Free Church Consultant & Associate Bible Teacher,
Radio Bible Class

"Most would agree that tragedy and pain are inherent in the human condition, and yet as Sam Kee masterfully illustrates within Hope Stands our God is both active and present throughout our seasons of despair. Using thoughtful Biblical exposition from the Gospel of John, the Author furnishes each reader with ten solid reasons to know with absolute certainty that in the midst of seemingly hopeless times the One who is hope Himself, our Lord Christ, is ever near! I therefore recommend this book very highly to all who find themselves in the dark valley of despair. In its pages they will undoubtedly discover Hope."

Michael Gleason
Campus Minister, Kent State University at Stark

"Pastor Kee has given even the most hopeless a reason for hope. Not a "wished-for" hope, but rather a Living Hope. Read to be encouraged, and then encourage someone else with this hope-giving book!"

Hutz H. Hertzberg
Executive Pastor, The Moody Church, Chicago, IL

Dedicated to Shanté and the boys

"Why are you weeping?"
~ John 20:15

"Blessed be the God and Father of our Lord Jesus Christ! According to his great mercy, he has caused us to be born again to a living hope through the Resurrection of Jesus Christ from the dead."
~ 1 Peter 1:3

With thee
Let me combine,
And feel this day thy victory:
For, if I imp my wing on thine,
Affliction shall advance the flight in me.
~ "Easter Wings" by George Herbert

7

Table of Contents

Foreword

Have you ever felt like your life was so messed up that nothing or no one could ever fix it? I have. From the earliest time I can remember, my life was a struggle for survival in a cold, cruel, and crowded world. As a child, impoverished, abused, and lonely, a dark cloak of despair seemed to suffocate me. Surrounded by ugliness, growing up, I wondered if things would ever get better. I wondered if anyone would stand up for me.

The day my father died, something inside of me died with him. His tragic death, when I was fifteen, destroyed every dream I had ever dreamed. I gave up on life because, for me, death seemed a better prospect than living some miserable existence. The cuts on my arms told the story of what was happening in my soul. I was bleeding out. Could anything or anyone hear me, help me, or heal me?

Eventually, I pulled a gun out from under my bed and put it up to my head with my finger on the trigger. That should have been my last day, but it wasn't. I was about to find out something that I had never been told- there's always another solution, you just have to wait for it. It will come, sometimes in the most unlikely way.

When I was seventeen, a visit from an uninvited guest changed everything for me. That visit, which consisted of nothing more than a simple prayer and an invitation to a church

9

service, would radically alter my entire destiny. A couple of weeks later the weight of my tears dropped me to my knees at the front of that woman's church. I met Jesus that day because when everyone else seemed to be running away, I found him standing up for me. The guilt, the addiction, the bitterness, and the pain all melted away in the experience of his presence.

Since that day I have been obsessed with telling everyone, everywhere about this Hope that stands. The work of my non-profit, Emerge, Inc., has given me a platform to do just that. Having now traveled across the country and spoken to more than 300,000 students, most of them in public high schools, I can tell you that hopelessness is pandemic. It knows no context. Individuals, families, and neighborhoods in urban, suburban, and rural communities suffer from its pervasive effects.

Loneliness, abandonment, and neglect fill our streets with an absence of hope. Like the sixteen year old gang member named Derek in Detroit who stood on the gym floor in his high school, thirty minutes before lunch, burying his head in my chest, his tears soaking my shirt. His father walked out on him and his mom. His deep longing for a sense of belonging led him down an angry road of violence and crime. Or, what about the seventeen year old girl named Julianne who stood in line for over an hour after I spoke in her high school, just to tell me her story. Her high school had been devastated with five suicides in a single year. Her brother was the first. Every student who took their life, thereafter, left her with the gruesome reality of living her brother's death all over again. I could feel the hurt in her eyes that day as her head collapsed into her hands, tears jumping through the gaps in her fingers. Their lives will never be the same because they found Hope standing in the midst of their struggle.

The beautiful thing about our gospel is this- Jesus gives us dignity in exchange for our despair. What would happen if this hope could spread like fire to the countless souls searching for more? Sam Kee gives us Ten Reasons to believe that it can, and that it must. Sam inspires and illuminates the resurrection with the promise that out of our tragedies we will emerge as trophies of His grace. He convinces us of that which has often been lost in the great stories of the resurrection, namely that we don't have to quit.

In Hope Stands, Sam makes the reality of the resurrection tangible and forces its implications on your conscience. Each of his ten reasons for not giving up will hit your soul with the force of sledge-hammer, shattering your sense of hopelessness. This generation desperately needs a book like this- theologically robust and wildly inspirational. Sam Kee brilliantly delivers both!

Without a single shred of doubt in my mind, Hope Stands will bring deep healing and help to all those who read it. Let this book create in you a new vision of the resurrection of Jesus. What you see when you look outside your window will never be the same and more importantly, neither will what you see when you look in the mirror.

Keith Robinson *is the Founder/President of a non-profit organization, Emerge, Inc. With a mission to bring healing to this generation by engaging them with a message of Hope and methods of help, Keith travels and speaks to more than 100,000 students each year across the nation. He is a motivational speaker and leader, combining the efforts of students, leaders, and churches for an outreach strategy called the Emerge Experience (www.emergexperience.com) and also leads the Young Adult Community at his home church, Bethel Temple Community Church, in Evansville, IN.*

Introduction

While I was preparing to speak at a weekend retreat for high school students, I suddenly felt burdened to make some significant changes. My assignment was to speak on John chapter twenty, but God seemed to be telling me to talk about suicide. I soon realized that both my sudden burden to address the issue of suicide and my assignment to speak on John twenty were not at odds with each other. In fact, I discovered that the stories of The Resurrection appearances in John twenty were the strongest sources of hope that I could offer. I titled my message for that Friday night "Hope Stands" and nervously wondered if such a message would be well received. I feared that I might be way off track by addressing the issue of suicide on a weekend retreat for high school students.

Right before I left for the retreat, I got a phone call from one of the youth ministers who was bringing a group of students to the retreat. "Sam," he said, "One of my students just committed suicide." After processing that news with the youth minister, I quickly understood that my sudden burden a day before to speak on suicide was more than a coincidence.

That night at the retreat I told hundreds of students about The Resurrection. I told them that they are never without hope so long as one person is standing up for them. Fighting tears, I spoke about suicide and acknowledged the tragedy that had just happened. I wanted every person in that room to know that they are never without hope.

The response was unexpected. By speaking about suicide,

I touched a nerve. So many students were struggling with despair and hopelessness. Spontaneously, they gathered around one another after the message and prayed for each other. They cried on each other and embraced each other. Several admitted that they wanted to give up on life. I had not anticipated that a group like this would wrestle with hopelessness so much.

A couple of days later, someone from the retreat contacted me. She told me quite simply, "You have to let the world know about the stand." Her point was clear. There are so many people who struggle with hopelessness; students, as well as adults. Hopelessness is not generational. Today, it is thick and wide, engulfing everyone. It is both a mood and a destination. But this person knew that we have a way to fight. We have Someone who is willing to stand up for us. The world has to hear about that.

This book is meant to give you hope. In its pages, you will find ten reasons why you must not give up. When you want to call it quits, I want you to know that hope is not gone. You have a reason to go on. In fact, you have ten solid reasons.

Notice I said that these are "solid" reasons. That is the difference that I am trying to make with this book. As we look for hope, plenty of people are offering it these days. There are writers, celebrities, and politicians. I have even seen upscale clothing companies scribbling the word "hope" on their products. Hope is definitely fashionable. It is the subject of books, speeches, music, and movies. Nonetheless, the hope that I have seen is not solid. It is more abstract, based on ideas rather than observations, on interpretation rather than history. It feels synthetic rather than organic. It is hope that has been assembled from the best pieces of humanity, working together to lift our spirits.

I do not want a synthetic hope. Something that is fabricated does not seem like it will sustain me when despair gets heavy and hard. I want organic hope. I want hope that grows up within my trial as a contradiction to my trial. I want hope that exists not because someone put it together, but because it was the last thing standing when everything else fell apart.

I do not want to imagine hope. I do not want to wish for hope. I want to see hope. I want to remember hope as an event, rather than as a set of advice. When I am in despair, I want hope to be as tangible as a man standing up in my living room. When I am in the trenches, I want to be able to see hope standing there, like a rock that will never go away, no matter how bad things get. I do not want to have to invent theories of hope, or remember clever acronyms or adjectives for hope. When tears cloud my eye, I want to see that one person is still there for me, no matter what.

That is why I am using a single story throughout this book. It is the story of Jesus' Resurrection as recorded by the Apostle John. It is found in John chapters twenty and twenty-one in the Bible. By using a real life story, I want to show you that hope is organic. It grows up within the situations we find ourselves. John's story also helps us to visualize hope. It is easier to remember a story than it is to remember an outline. Hope is not the product of a cleverly argued thesis; it is a historical event—a real story in real life. Hope is not uncertain but certain. We are not waiting for something good to happen, hope has already happened. It is a treasure for us to discover.

Even more, hope will not leave. It remains standing. Nothing can defeat it. John's story shows us that hope can stand up to anything. This means that you are never without it. This book is meant to give you hope when you need it the most.

This book is for those who are waiting to see the doctor at their cancer appointment. It is for the spouse whose husband walked out on the family after twenty years. It is for the young man who tried to hang himself and the young woman who took too many pills. It is for the person who keeps cutting herself in order to feel a release from the stress. It is for the girl with the eating disorder who keeps questioning her worth.

It is for the person on the park bench, who stares off into the distance, wondering if there is one good reason to keep living. It is for the person who is alone, because his spouse suddenly passed away. It is for the one who is searching for his purpose in life and for the one who needs something solid to stand upon. It is for you. I want you to know that you can find hope in your situation.

I am not naive, nonetheless. I know that the issue of suicide is very complex, involving biology, heredity, and environment. I do not pretend to offer a complete solution to this multifaceted issue. Medicine needs to work in concert with counseling in most cases. Professionals need to be contacted when suicide is a threat. This book is not meant to take the place of crisis intervention. But it is aimed at helping with our despair.

Maybe you are not at the point of wanting to take your life. But you still need courage to go forward. You still need to find hope. In these chapters, I will present ten reasons why you should have hope in your life. Here are ten things I want you to know. First, something good is happening in your life. Second, your greatest enemy has been defeated. Third, you are loved. Fourth, someone is standing up for you (this is the crucial reason that illuminates all of the others). Fifth, you are released from sorrow. Sixth, you are released from fear. Seventh, you are released from doubt. Eighth, your future is not failure. Ninth, your purpose is restored. Tenth, you are essential.

When Jesus Christ stood up from the grave on the third day, he released a power to all those who would follow him. The resurrection releases us from the emotional conditions that trap us.

Once we are released, the resurrection gives us a purpose in life and a mission. This book takes the resurrection into the center of the human experience and detonates it.

To the person who demands, "Give me one good reason to go on," I have ten.

Reason #1:

Something Good Is Happening

"Now on the first day of the week Mary Magdalene came to the tomb early, while it was still dark, and saw that the stone had been taken away from the tomb...[The disciples] did not understand the Scripture, that he must rise from the dead."
~ John 20:1 and 9

The Moon

The moon is a witness in the dark. I have learned to see the moon in a new way because of a poem called The Bridge by Henry Wadsworth Longfellow.[1] In the poem, Longfellow wonders how many thousands of "care-encumbered men" have walked on this bridge and gazed out into the ocean, questioning where life's answers would come from. How many other burdened people have "stood on that bridge at midnight" with tears in their eyes? How many other broken souls have wished that the ocean would "bear me away on its bosom?" How many others have stood in this place with troubles that

[1] *Henry Wadsworth Longfellow, Longfellow: Poems and Other Writings, ed. J. D. McClatchy (New York: Literary Classics of the United States, 2000), 45-46.*

17

"seemed greater than I could bear?" Ironically, as he stands on the bridge at midnight, the church behind him is dark. That is when he notices the moon:

> *The moon and its broken reflection*
> *And its shadows shall appear,*
> *As the symbol of love in heaven,*
> *And its wavering image here.*

When you are on the bridge at midnight, no matter how dark and dramatic life appears, there is hope, buried in the darkness, just as the moon is buried in the night. Longfellow sees the moon "as the symbol of love in heaven." Love is out there, he believes. Even though it is dark in his world, he knows that light still exists in another world. Just because it is night here does not mean that there is no sun. The sun still exists. Light still exists. Love still lives. "The moon and its broken reflection" prove this. For the moon carries the promise of dawn.

When I look at the moon, I see hope. Though surrounded by black, the presence of this single light shows me that hope is not dead. I know that there is still "love in heaven," though it is cold and dark here. For the moon bears the reflection of the sun, as the chief mirror in the sky. When I look at the moon, I see that morning is on its way. I need to wait on the bridge just a little longer.

There is a double-reflection here. Sometimes we do not see the reflection of the sun's light directly on the moon. Instead, we see it on the waves below. When we cannot even lift our heads to the sky, we are still able to see the moon's "broken reflection" on the trembling waters beneath us. This gives me hope, too. The moon leaves its witness on the waters as a "wavering image here." This means that hope is possible even for those who cannot lift their heads.

As we begin the story of the stand, we begin with the moon, not the sun. We begin on the bridge, "while it was still dark" (John 20:1). We begin with a wavering image and a double-reflection. The story of the stand does not begin in strength, but in weakness. We start at a cemetery, not at a banquet. We start with questions and not answers. We start with problems and misunderstanding rather than solutions and certainty. We start with the broken reflection of hope floating timidly on the tide beneath us. Though it looks fragile and thin, its wavering image still stands. Hope is out there and is on its way, whether we realize it or not.

Perspective

Do you know the difference between subjectivity and objectivity? Subjectivity is when you make a conclusion about the world that is based too much on your own personal impressions or feelings. Objectivity is when you try to make judgments about the world based on external facts and unbiased observations.

It helps to put these terms into a context, like music lyrics. Some songs are very subjective. They express one's feelings and experiences from a personal point of view. The self is the subject of the song. Other songs are objective. These songs take an outside perspective and record an event that happened. These songs tell a story, in other words. Not every song is perfectly subjective or perfectly objective. The two categories bleed into one another. When I tell a story, it is still I the subject who tell it.

Events and their interpretation fall prey to the interaction of subjectivity and objectivity. This is especially true when events are either very positive or very negative. It is a slippery slope. When an event is negative, it is easy to find another negative. Soon, the negative events begin to pile up, and it seems unlikely they will ever stop. Soon, the glass begins to look half empty, always. Subjective negativity takes over and we lose sight of anything positive. Even if something positive did happen, our subjectivity stains our objective ability to recognize it.

Nothing Was Going Right

Have you ever had one of those days when it seemed like everything was going wrong? From the moment you stepped out of bed, life malfunctioned: you cannot find clean clothes to wear, you are out of milk for breakfast, you are late for work, your boss starts nagging as soon as you get in the door, you forgot your homework assignment, you are fighting with your friends, your family does not understand, you fail at a task, you are let go from your job, and on it goes.

Once I tried to fix a ball joint in my car. On the surface, it did not look like too big of a job. I just had to loosen one bolt and then pop out the ball joint. I thought it would take an hour to do. It did not take an hour or even two hours. It took me three days to remove the ball joint! I later learned that mankind has invented something called a "ball joint separator," which is a special tool used to remove ball joints. I was told (after I already removed it), "There's no way you'll be able to remove the ball joint without a separator!" Now they tell me. But in the process of trying to remove the ball joint, I broke several tools (including some of my neighbor's) and four other adjacent car parts! Trying to fix one problem, I created several other problems. Nothing was going right!

There was a day one winter when nothing was going right for my friend John. In the morning, he went to be with a family member who was ill. That was quite hard. Then there was a severe snowstorm, during which John got in an accident. Power lines fell down just near his car as he was dodging another car sliding in his direction. When he finally arrived at his office, he got news that the family member he visited earlier had just died. Later that day, as he was telling his wife the news of the death, she received a phone call from her brother. She was shocked to learn that her father had just suddenly passed away. That was the second family death of the day. In the middle of all that, the plumbers called John to ask how he wanted to pay for the $10,000 plumbing bill for the emergency trenching and re-piping work they were finishing up in his basement. It seemed like nothing good was happening.

That is where the first followers of Jesus were. Nothing was going their way. *They had just witnessed the death of their close friend, Jesus.* That is nothing for us to read too quickly or brush to the side. They witnessed their close friend die. Have you ever seen a close friend or family member die? Have you ever stood by his or her side, helplessly trying to be helpful? They are suffering terribly and there is not a thing you can do about it. Your heart leaps out of your chest for your loved one, only to fall painfully to the floor.

The first followers of Jesus did not watch a "sterile" death, either—not that there is such a thing. He did not die quietly by laying in a hospital bed to the rhythm of monitors and oxygen machines. It was not a peaceful death; rather, it was a violent one. Jesus was tortured first; beaten with rods and scourged with whips. His body was laid open from head to toe by a cat-a-nine-tails laced with bone, metal, and glass. His beard was pulled out by mockers. His face was coated with obnoxious spit and his soul with outrageous slander. His feet and hands were nailed with iron spikes. His head was punctured with the ten-inch thorns of a date palm, shaped into the form of a sardonic crown. He writhed in pain. His body was hung cruelly on a cross, only to be plunged into asphyxiation and ultimately death. *That is what his friends had to go through.* They even had to watch the executioners thrust a spear through his side, just to make sure that the death sentence was complete.

No wonder the first followers of Jesus were hiding in their homes immediately after that Friday afternoon, April 3, 30 AD. No wonder they wept. No wonder they feared. No wonder they doubted. What was there left to hope for now?

Funerals and burials help bring closure to grieving. Mourners have depended on these ceremonies from the beginning. When Mary wanted to complete the burial rites for Jesus, she discovered that his body was missing. She feared that someone had taken away their friend. On top of all she went through, now she cannot even find Jesus' body to give him a descent burial. It seemed like nothing was going right!

Mary finds two other followers of Jesus, Peter and John. Peter and John run to the tomb to verify Mary's report. They, too, cannot find the body. This means not only that someone stole away their friend, which is a horrible thought, but also that their lives were in danger. They knew the rumors that would start. The authorities would soon accuse the followers of Jesus of stealing the body, causing the followers to be in danger from the government, as well. No wonder they ran home! They were scared for their lives. Nothing was going right for the first followers of Jesus.

Everything Was Going Right

In the same breath, it can be said that everything was going right. Despite the torture, death, alleged grave robbery, and threats from the authorities, life turned the corner. They were standing on the edge of the single most important event that this world has ever known. They were walking in the dirt and dust of life's greatest miracle. In the midst of their tears crouched triumph, like a tiger waiting to pounce. As the dawn was driving away the dark, Jesus was driving away death. In the words of John Donne, God the Father was proclaiming, "Death, thou shalt die!"[2] Indeed, as Jesus stood up after his own massacre, God said, "Death, thou art dead!"

That is the single greatest feat this world has ever known. There are no competitors. All of life and history, kingdoms and

[2] John Donne, *The Collected Poems of John Donne*, ed. Roy Booth (England: Wordsworth Editions Limited, 1994), 251.

powers, had been searching for and waiting for this moment. Humans have covered the earth in search of immortality. Nations have raged against each other in pursuit of the best life, the most peace, and the greatest justice. Human history has been and will always be about the pursuit of life and the avoidance of death. Every culture has this question at its foundation, "What will bring us life?" Life is the default of our existence.

That is what God just did; he turned the tables on death. As we will learn in the next chapter, God undid death. God caused one person in the pool of humanity to be released. The walls have been torn down. It is just a matter of time before we all can be set free.

Everything was going wrong; everything was going right. In the presence of personal pains and emotions, an external victory was won. This was an objective fact, which was happening alongside of the subjective struggles of each person. Jesus was alive. Death was defeated and the new era had dawned. If one person stood up after death, now all people can. This was news that would change everything.

They Did Not Even Know It
And the followers of Jesus did not even realize it. They stood on the bridge at midnight and did not apprehend the significance of the moon. Drowned in their own emotions, the external facts did not register in their expectations. Do not get me wrong; they had good reasons for missing it. After all, resurrections do not happen every day. No one expected Jesus to rise from the dead. Culturally, the Greeks did not have a place in their philosophy for a bodily resurrection. Since the body was considered "bad," it was unthinkable for the pure soul to be reunited with the evil body after death. The goal of life was to be freed from the body, not to be trapped by the body for all eternity, as it would be in a bodily-resurrected state. The Jews,

on the other hand, did not believe in this sort of resurrection. Some Jews held that there would be a general resurrection of all God's people at the end of the age, when the Messiah ruled his kingdom. But they did not expect one person to rise from the grave way ahead of time.[3]

Besides these reasons, the Messiah, which Jesus claimed he was, was not supposed to be defeated, as Jesus was. The Messiah was supposed to be the king who would never be defeated, which is what qualified him to be the Messiah in the first place. But this guy, Jesus, was obviously defeated. He did not beat the Romans; the Romans beat him. He was no true Messiah, but an imposter. So they thought.

Because of the prevailing view on the Resurrection and the messianic expectations, the first followers of Jesus were caught off guard, to say the least. They did not expect Jesus to rise from the dead. That is why they did not see the objective miracle when it happened. The passage says that,

For as yet they did not understand the scripture, that he must rise from the dead. ~ John 20:9

Even the Scriptures pointed to a bodily resurrection of the Messiah, but they did not understand their own teaching.

Here is the lesson: in the midst of everything pointing in the wrong direction, the resurrection happens. The resurrection is a total reversal of our expectations. It is a total undoing of hopelessness. In the midst of the suffering, the objective fact of the resurrection emerges. It rises as the sun, quietly on the horizon of our human darkness. It does not make any noise. It does not announce itself. It does not prepare us. It does not ask our opinion or preference. It just happens, whether we know it or not, whether we expect it or not, whether we are ready or not. Here it comes. Hope is here.

[3] N. T. Wright, *The Resurrection of the Son of God* (Minneapolis: Fortress Press, 2003).

Do Not Give Up Now

I can relate to the first followers of Jesus. Sometimes it seems like everything is going wrong and nothing is going right. But we must not give up, even though we scramble on the slippery slope of subjectivity. We must not call it quits. Though we are on the edge, let this thought jar us back: something good is happening, even though our negative expectations keep us from seeing it. Quietly in the background of your life, one man is standing up for you. Did you know that? Did you know that right now something is going right for you?

Something good is happening, I promise. Do not give up now. Do not fail to see that the miracle of life you have been waiting for has already happened. Let me point out one more part of the story. On the one hand, the first followers of Jesus did not understand what was happening. On the other hand, one of the followers did. It says that one of the disciples "saw and believed" (John 20:8). This follower, whose name was John, knew that the body was not stolen. John trusted that God had a hand in this. John believed that Jesus was alive, so far as we can tell. John was the exception.

As I close this chapter, let me offer you some support. Right now, you may not believe good will come; you might have an outlook more like that of Peter, Mary, or the other followers. You may not see it yet, and that is okay, because I will be John for you. Let me believe, even when you cannot and together we will discover nine more reasons why we must not give up.

Reason #2:

You Are Freed from Your Greatest Enemy

"Now on the first day of the week Mary Magdalene came to the tomb early, while it was still dark, and saw that the stone had been taken away from the tomb. So she ran and went to Simon Peter and the other disciple, the one whom Jesus loved, and said to them, "They have taken the Lord out of the tomb, and we do not know where they have laid him." So Peter went out with the other disciple, and they were going toward the tomb. Both of them were running together, but the other disciple outran Peter and reached the tomb first. And stooping to look in, he saw the linen cloths lying there, but he did not go in. Then Simon Peter came, following him, and went into the tomb. He saw the linen cloths lying there, and the face cloth, which had been on Jesus' head, not lying with the linen cloths but folded up in a place by itself. Then the other disciple, who had reached the tomb first, also went in, and he saw and believed; for as yet they did not understand the Scripture, that he must rise from the dead. Then the disciples went back to their homes." ~ John 20:1-10

27

Burial Clothes

I hate burial clothes. I have been to a lot of funerals and the burial clothes always have the same effect on me. I get angry. They seem to be mocking the living. I know that this could be a sensitive subject and I realize that there are no other alternatives—we need to make our deceased loved ones look nice for the funeral—but hear me out. Picture the scene: Grandma Jane is lying still in the casket, wearing a beautiful blue dress with a floral pattern. Maybe her favorite large brimmed sun hat is tucked neatly in her hands, as if she is still able to hold it. Her glasses are still on and her hair is fixed nicely. She even has on make-up. Most everyone comments, probably because they do not know what else to say, "How lovely Grandma Jane looks!" "She always did look so good in that dress."

Not me. I get angry. The dress laughs at me and says, "Ha! Look who I have!" "I've got Grandma Jane and she looks so good!" "She looks just like she did when she was alive!"

The grave clothes try to make the situation look normal. But the situation is not normal. Grandma cannot see out of her glasses. The flowers on her dress do not mean that she is alive and well and flourishing. It is a disguise. Nothing is right about the situation. A happy dress will not change the fact that she is no longer with us. The clothes mock.

Grave clothes represent our attempt to make a bad situation feel better. But, if we are honest, it does not work. The grave clothes only highlight the fact that death is not normal. We dress up death, desperately trying to make death live. We clothe death, but death does not go away. It is still there, only now it is wearing a silly blue dress. I am quite sure that death has been laughing for centuries at our efforts to hide it.

Though our efforts have been to hide or disguise death, we have not been able to make it go away. Death has always won. Grave clothes remind us of that, even as they try to make us feel better.

In the first century, the dead would be wrapped in grave clothes in the form of strips of linen. Dozens of pounds of spices would be placed within the strips. This was an effort to disguise the obvious and keep death hidden from view. Metaphorically, just as the grave clothes wrap around the body, so does death have its grip wrapped around us. Neither the grave clothes nor death will let go. They are here to stay.

Rewind

What if we could rewind life to a point before death? Would that free us from the grave? We long to do this. Our bones ache for just one more chance. We often want to rewind events and do them over again. We often desire to return to a more pleasant time, before the pain struck. We often want to go back before the disease took over or the relationship rotted. We want to spend just one more hour with our loved one, just one more chance to do the right thing. We all long to go back in time.

What would life look like if we could simply rewind it? It seemed like Lazarus was able to do this. In John 11, we learn that the man Lazarus dies and is placed in a tomb for four days. Lazarus is completely dead. Then along comes Jesus and orders him to come out of the tomb—and Lazarus does! Eventually, in the years to come, though Lazarus had cheated death, Lazarus would die again. Why? Because Lazarus was placed right back on the same old pathway of life: the pathway that leads to death. We are all on it. Lazarus did not get off this pathway, but was rewound to an earlier point on it. Jesus rewound Lazarus' life so that he could live in an earlier and healthier version of his body. Eventually, nonetheless, since he was on the pathway toward death, Lazarus would face death once again. He would eventually be placed in the same exact tomb a second time. In other words, Lazarus would be wrapped in the grave clothes again. The grave clothes, once again, would have the last laugh. After all, when Lazarus came out of the tomb, the grave clothes still clung menacingly to him, for he would again need them someday soon.

Undo

It does no good to rewind life. This is merely a temporary solution. Rewinding life would not stop problems from occurring; it would not change the path for which your life is destined. You need a better solution, which we find in John 20:1-10. This passage does not simply back up the tragic story to an earlier point in the tragic story—for that would not free us from the heartbreaking plot. Rather, this passage does something completely different.

Every detail of the story in John 20:1-10 points not to a rewinding of life, but to an undoing of death. The passage takes us out of death's backyard and gives us a new yard to play in. Consider five truths from the passage:

It was the first day of the week.

It is no mistake that John tells us that it was the first day of the week (John 20:1). John could have said, "It was the third day after the crucifixion." But he does not. Then John emphasizes, "it was still dark" (John 20:1). What is John getting at? Since the first words of his story, John has been attempting to retell the first book of the Bible, Genesis. John begins his story with these haunting words, "In the beginning…" (John 1:1). John wants his reader to remember how God first created the heavens and the earth out of the darkness. Now John brings his readers back to that "first day" and the "darkness" from which new life came. John wants us to see a whole new Genesis—a whole new beginning. Life is not just rewinding to an earlier point. Life is starting over from scratch. The resurrection means that the old is redone and not just relived.

30

The stone had been taken away.

When Mary arrives at the tomb, she was quite surprised to see that the stone had already been rolled away. She is so surprised that it sends her running to tell the others. This portrait of a grave standing open, unaided by human hands and surprising to human eyes, points to the revolutionary work of God.

John wants us to see that God did this. God rolled away the stone. God surprised the human, in this case, Mary. All graves stand open before our Mighty God. The grave cannot keep its door shut in the presence of God's power. God does not turn back time and rescue Jesus off of the cross, before he dies. Rather, God invades time and rescues Jesus out of the grave, after he dies. Again, the human storyline is not backed-up, but invaded. God undoes the death that was done. God opens that which humans shut. The grave stands mouth open and aghast when God comes to rescue humanity, starting with his Son. As a later biblical author attests, those who are "in Christ" will also be rescued by God (Colossians. 3:1-4).

The tomb was empty because the body was gone.

The body is gone. This has been the assumption and the big news from the beginning. Everyone knew it and no one argued against it. Even Jesus' enemies assumed the body was gone. For they do not give answers about why the body is really there, but about why the body is really missing. They assumed it was missing and merely said, "The disciples stole the body." Whether it was stolen or not is not the point; the point is that the body was gone.

The tomb is empty; the grave is vacant; and there is no death inside of it. Death is missing; death is gone; and death is no more. That is the astounding conclusion of the empty tomb. That is the big news that the world has been waiting to hear. Death went out of business; its residence is empty.

31

This is not the end of life, but the start of something new. Jesus started a revolution of life. Soon others would follow in his steps, conquering that which has never been conquered. The empty tomb meant triumph. Somebody finally triumphed over humankind's ugliest enemy.

The grave clothes were left behind in an unexpected way.

For the unnamed disciple, who most likely was John himself,[1] the sight of the grave clothes was the climax. To understand John's excitement, let us recall the difference between the rewinding of Lazarus' life and the undoing of Jesus' death. When Lazarus came out of the grave, he was still wearing his grave clothes. Lazarus, though resuscitated, did not pass permanently through death. Lazarus did not penetrate through his grave clothes. Death still clung to him. And eventually, death would cling to him once again.

This was not the case with Jesus. Jesus did not come out of the grave wearing his grave clothes; they were left behind. Jesus passed right through them in the same way he passed right through the walls of the disciple's home later in John 20. The grave clothes could not keep him bound. Death could not keep its grip on Jesus. Jesus passed through death and its mocking costume.

If Jesus had resuscitated, then he would have worn the grave clothes out of the tomb, like Lazarus did. He would not have left them behind in such an orderly way. In addition, if grave robbers came and stole the body, they would have stolen the grave clothes, too. They would not have taken them off the body and left them behind, carrying away a naked corpse. The grave clothes and spices within them were the most valuable things in the tomb. They surely would not have left behind the valuables if they were robbers.

Thus, when John saw this, he believed (John 20:8). The

[1] D. A. Carson, *The Gospel According to John* (Leicester, England: Apollos, 1991), 68.

grave clothes were lying there as if nothing had ever happened. Mary, Peter, and John did not enter the tomb and see a bloody body wrapped in grave clothes. They did not see an empty tomb, void of even grave clothes. They did not even see a disorderly scene of grave clothes, strewn throughout the tomb, as if to give evidence of foul play. Rather, they saw the defeated grave clothes, no longer proudly holding another victim. The scene is tranquil, as if nothing had ever happened. The body was gone. The grave clothes were robbed of their purpose. John knew that there was no longer any need for the grave clothes. That is when he believed that death had been undone.

There were multiple witnesses.

This was such an unbelievable event that John knew he needed to reassure his readers. That is why he emphasizes the fact that there were multiple witnesses: himself, a disciple named Peter, and Mary. Thus his readers could be confident that this historical claim was verifiable, by two men and a woman, no less. In ancient times, at least two men were needed to support such claims. By naming multiple known witnesses, doubters could easily seek out and question them and hear their firsthand testimony.

Belief

John believes not because life makes sense, but because the body is missing. John bases his faith not on what has been done to his life, but what has been undone. John was wounded. His friend had been executed. He had plenty of reason to despair and give up hope, for life did not make sense. He even says that the Scriptures did not make sense (John 20:9). The fact that John ran and then hesitated to go into the tomb shows that his emotions were surging. As we will see later, these resurrection accounts show multiple people whose emotional states were off balanced.

John does not base his faith off of feeling. He does not base his faith off of religious history or tradition either, for he did not understand the Scriptures. John bases his faith off of the scene before his eyes. Does John fully understand what happened? Does he completely comprehend that Jesus rose bodily from the grave? Of course not! So what does John believe?

John believes that Jesus was right after all! Jesus was not a condemned criminal in God's eyes. Jesus was not cursed by the Creator of the universe, as many thought. For only a condemned and cursed criminal would be crucified. When John saw that God had undone the crucifixion, John realized that God had said "Yes!" to Jesus' life. God accepted Jesus. God vindicated his life, ministry, and death. If God was pleased with Jesus, then John was pleased with Jesus, too. John believed that Jesus really was who he claimed to be; the Resurrection was proof of God's blessed acceptance of his true Son.

Here is the point. God does not need to do something spectacular in your life to give you hope. God does not need to do something to give you a reason to go on. We only need to look to what God has undone to have hope. The rest of life may not make sense to us. It may take us a while to see how it all fits together. But at least we can be sure that God has begun to undo life as we know it—the gears are in motion! It started with Jesus, when his life was undone. You can be sure that God can undo your life, as well.

That gives us rock solid hope. Nothing can take that away. God could give us extended life, but that could be taken away. God could give us a better friend or spouse, but those can be taken away. God could give us more loving parents, but those, too, can leave. That which is undone will last. To be undone is to start a whole new project.

Right now, those who put their faith in Jesus, like John, have begun a whole new irrevocable life. It is a life that is not tainted by death or loss. It is an existence that begins with life and ends with glory.

We want to give up on life when life is not working. The resurrection gives us new categories. God undoes that which is undoing us. When pain undoes us, God undoes pain. Then he puts us in a new house so that we can play in a new yard and be a part of a new family. We are headed not toward death, but life—real life. God flips the whole thing on its head. The resurrected Jesus looks deeply into your eyes and says, "Do not give up on life, for I have already given up on death." There is a seed of hope waiting for you to discover. It is the hope that comes from knowing that life will not come completely undone for you, for Jesus undid that which was undoing us. In other words, life is always standing at the end of your trial. Yes, we will still have trials and pains in this life, but ultimately, they will be undone. They will not have the last laugh.

Do not give up. God has already put to death your greatest enemy. If your greatest enemy has been undone, then you can get through anything. You can make it through whatever you are dealing with right now. Your greatest foe has been defeated; your greatest fear stands empty. The mocking grave clothes have been undressed and humiliated.

Splitting the Adam

He could only say a few words when he called from the hospital. "Cindy just died." I was soon on my way. They were close family friends of ours.

Standing bedside of Cindy at the hospital, a single verse of Scripture penetrated my thoughts, "For you are dust, and to dust you shall return" (Genesis 3:19). I did not welcome the verse, but it did not ask me for permission. The words first spoken by God to Adam and Eve would not leave my mind. Though I hated the scene before me, I knew that dust had just returned to dust.

We are all marching toward dust. We are dust merging into dust. The categories of dust are separate so long as we are alive, like two poles. But the more we live, the closer the poles get to each other. Dust creeps closer to dust. One day, whether we like it or not, the two poles will merge together and become one. Dust will return to dust. No matter how hard we try to keep ourselves separate from death, one day we will merge together with it. We will become dust.

That is the thing that struck me the most when standing bedside of my friend. Cindy became death. Death was no longer separate from her, off in the distance. Death had merged with her life. She was death. The categories had become one. She was both herself and death at the same time. She was as still as the dust from which she came, for she was the dust from which she came.

One day, I will merge with the dust, too. Death will not just be something outside of me, but death will be me. I am not sure when it will happen. It could be today. Today could be the day when death eclipses my life and I return to that from which I was born. Today I could be as still as the earth beneath my feet.

"Adam" literally means "earth." The first human, Adam, came from the earth; and he returned to the earth, as the dust returned to dust. It is sobering to live with this knowledge. We are all Adam, bits of earth headed back to bits of earth. For now we roam, achieve, seek, ache, love, cry, run, and rest. Someday we will stop completely. Someday we will freeze back into that from which we came. We will be as still as silence, totally merged with death and dust. There will not be an ounce of life left in us. The two will become one.

No matter what I said or what I did, I would not be able to separate Cindy from death. The process was complete. Nor was there any human invention that might extract the dust of her life from the dust of her death. Standing before her, I was sobered by the fact that death had won once again. I had no remedies; I was powerless. This was more than a nail that needed to be pulled from some wood; these were two ingredients that had turned into something completely different.

We are all on the march toward dust. We will all be Cindy one day. The question before us is, "What will be able to separate the dust from the dust?" We need to find something or somebody who can un-grip us from the fist of death. Can anything or anybody unhinge a body from dust when it has already merged with it?

Every pain we go through is one step closer to dust. Every sin that is done against us is one step closer to dust. Every sin that we commit is one step closer to dust. Hurt and evil are evidences of the merge. They are reminders of where we are headed. That is why sin is such a big deal to God, because it drags us to our knees and forces us into the dust—literally.

Your greatest enemy is not an adversary on earth. Your greatest enemy is neither your personal failures nor any obstacles in your life. Your greatest enemy is death, for it is the greatest offense to life. Nothing will do more damage to your life than death. Nothing will cause more pain to you and those around you than death.

When Jesus stood up from the grave he walked out on death and left it in the dust. The second reason why you must not give up is that your greatest enemy has been defeated. The Resurrection pries us out of the hands of death and sets us free.

Effective Today

The resurrection attacks the dust at two points in our existence. On the one hand, the resurrection becomes effective upon our death, after the merge. It pries death from life, separating that which was inseparable. This means that it undoes the consequences of our sin. Though sin pushes us to dust, the resurrection pushes us to life. The cross is between the two.

Jesus hangs between life and death, forgiving the penalty of our sin on the cross and reversing the power of our sin by the resurrection.

On the other hand, the resurrection goes to work today. Before I merge with death, the resurrection of Jesus Christ gives life, today. When Jesus rose from the grave, when the "Adam" was split, a great power was released. This power goes out from Jesus and is channeled through the Holy Spirit to his followers. The followers of Jesus can taste the fruit of the resurrection today and do not have to wait until death.

What does this fruit taste like? The dust of sorrow is changed to the fruit of purpose. The dust of fear is turned into the fruit of joy. The dust of doubt is turned into the fruit of belief. The dust of failure is turned into the fruit of success. The dust of regret is turned into the fruit of restoration. The dust of envy is turned into the fruit of essentiality. In chapters five through ten, we will see the resurrection go to work in each of these conditions of dust. Today, God wants to take the resurrection into the center of your being and detonate it.

But before we consider these astonishing effects of the resurrection, we must first be rooted in love.

Reason #3:

You Are Loved

When the Jews who were with her in the house, consoling her, saw Mary rise quickly and go out, they followed her, supposing that she was going to the tomb to weep there. Now when Mary came to where Jesus was and saw him, she fell at his feet, saying to him, "Lord, if you had been here, my brother would not have died." When Jesus saw her weeping, and the Jews who had come with her also weeping, he was deeply moved in his spirit and greatly troubled. And he said, "Where have you laid him?" They said to him, "Lord, come and see." Jesus wept. So the Jews said, "See how he loved him!"
~ John 11:31-36

Glass Heart

A church in Ohio asked me to speak at a men's breakfast. Typically at these men's gatherings, men are challenged to be men, be leaders, and be courageous. One usually leaves with a fresh, motivational "locker room" message to spur on his manliness for the rest of his life—or at least until the next month's men's breakfast. But I took a different approach. My three themes were: be yourself, be loved, and be passionate. These men did not have to put on football pads in order to listen to my message. I wanted them to leave with a sense of the pride and unconditional love God holds for them.

After I spoke, as the men were clearing out, one older gentleman approached me. He had wild gray hair and bowed legs. He was small and stocky and walked with a limp. Right away he said to me, "I used to wrestle for my school; and I never lost a match!" His voice was forceful, scratchy, and proud. I nodded with approval. During my message, I had told stories of when I used to wrestle.

Then the man held out his hand to me. When I tried to shake his hand, I noticed an object in it. He was holding a four-inch glass heart. It was composed of red, white, and pink stained glass, carefully held together by silver metal. "Here," the man said, "Have this. I made it for you."

I took the glass heart from him and held it carefully in my hand. I examined it. It was petite and beautiful, unlike this rough man standing before me. On a red piece of glass at the bottom of the heart were two letters: GZ. This man had engraved his initials on the glass heart he gave to me. After the man left, the host of the breakfast approached me and asked, "Do you know who that was?" I told him that I did not. The host told me the man's name and then said, "He's a millionaire. He owns large chain of stores."

I slipped the glass heart in my jacket pocket and headed for my car. As the day's activities ensued, I forgot all about the man's heart in my pocket. When I arrived at home late that night, I flung my jacket over my shoulder as I was walking to my front door. As I did that, I heard an object fall on my concrete driveway. Looking down, I saw that the glass heart had fallen out of my pocket and onto the ground. At that moment I realized what a dangerous thing it is to give your heart away.

We Keep Giving Our Hearts Away

A lot could go wrong when you give your "glass heart" away. One could break it, neglect it, forget about it, or abuse it. This man had entrusted me with his heart. He was venturing risk when he gave it to me. I had a vulnerable part of him. In a sense, I had power over him by the mere fact that I held his fragile heart in my hands.

We have all given our hearts away. We have all entrusted our glass heart into the hands of another. Some of our hearts have been broken and some have been abused. Some have been neglected. Some of us have given our hearts away to those who have genuinely loved us and cared for us—our hearts were safe in their hands.

Whether we have had good or bad experiences, whether our hearts were cared for or crushed, we keep doing it. Some of us have learned to be more careful with whom we entrust our hearts. Some of us are reckless with our hearts. Some of us are barely holding on; our hearts are cracked or broken, as we try to get the pieces of our lives back together.

We long to be whole so that we can do it again, so that we can give our heart away one more time. We hope that this will be the person who finally cares for us, as we want. Are we merely dumb creatures? We endanger our hearts over and over again. Why? Because we all long to be loved. We are hardwired for loving relationships; where another accepts us for whom we are and makes us better with his or her love. And we will keep on giving our hearts away until we find the hands that will bring healing rather than hurt.

Gods and Humans

The ancient Greeks believed that the gods did not and would not love humans. Thinkers such as Aristotle taught that the pagan gods would not risk giving their hearts away to mere mortals; divinity would not mix with depravity. After all, why would a god choose to get his or her heart broken by mere creatures? The gods only thought of themselves and did not go outside of themselves to care for and think of mortals. They could not have personal affections or interactions with mortals. They could not return emotional love to us or get involved with us. That would be too risky for any respectable god to do.

Thus for centuries humans have believed in distant, cold gods. When it comes to divinity, there cannot be an emotional connection. Humanity cannot engage divinity on a feeling-level. The gods cannot be impassioned, nor do they desire to get involved with our mess. The gods are not near emotionally, but far. Even worse, they are not even interested. This means that any relationship we have with a god must be based on fear. Humanity must appease the wrath of the gods. We must do whatever it takes to keep the gods happy. We walk on spiritual eggshells. We make sacrifice after sacrifice to manipulate deity—not so the god will swap feelings with us, but so the god will "put out" for us. "If I keep my god happy, then maybe he'll bless me. If I make incredible sacrifices to this god, then perhaps she'll perform for me." Humans have related to deity on this level for thousands of years. The gods serve one purpose: to come around only when help is needed, or asked for.

Such a view keeps God at a convenient distance. We no longer expect a relationship with God, but a contract. "I will do this and God will do this." Simple: no mess, no risk, no love.

That system seemed to work until God showed up in the human form of Jesus. God sent his love to us in flesh and blood, handing over his glass heart when he entrusted his Son into our hands. Jesus was God, born of Mary and Joseph around 3 B.C. He lived out God's passion for all of creation for 33 years, dying on a dark day in April. Jesus was a walking, talking glass heart. God's initials were engraved on his being. God gave us his love not in some sterile heavenly order, but in our infected earthly disorder.

We read about a profound instance of God's love in John

11. Let's take a moment away from John 20 in order to grasp the vast dimensions of God's love. My aim in sharing this is to help you see that your Maker profoundly and deeply loves you. This love, furthermore, is expressed by the Resurrection.

See How He Loves

Mary fell at Jesus' feet and said, "Lord, if you had been here, my brother would not have died" (John 11:32). Mary was weeping; Jesus was late. He could have been there earlier, as Mary said, but Jesus intentionally waited two days to come in order to ensure that Lazarus would be dead. Jesus did this because he loved Lazarus and his family. "Now Jesus loved Martha and her sister and Lazarus. So when he heard that he was ill, he stayed two days longer in the place where he was" (John 11:5-6). It seems that Lazarus' death had to be a factor in the full expression of Jesus' love for this family. Lazarus had to die so that Jesus might show how profoundly his love can change someone's life. Lazarus had to die in order for "resurrection" to enter the equation of this situation. Jesus was about to raise his friend from the dead as one of the ways of expressing his love for him (John 11:43-44).

Nonetheless, though Jesus knew that he would bring "resurrection" into this hopeless situation, he did not desist from entering their grief.

When Jesus saw her weeping, and the Jews who had come with her also weeping, he was deeply moved in his spirit and greatly troubled. - *John 11:33*

Their grief was important to Jesus. Jesus did not simply brush their grief to the side with one stupendous miracle. Instead, he acknowledged it and participated in it. He took time to show them that he cared and to validate their emotions.

Your grief is important to Jesus. Your tears provoke his tears and he wants to enter your pain and suffering, too. He

43

wants to participate with you on every level of your situation. God does not show up just in order to do the miracles. God shows up before the miracle, when we cannot see through our tears. When you are blind and confused, God is there. Do not look for him as "the light at the end of the tunnel." Look for him in the tunnel with you.

This is exactly what the Greek gods of old were trying to avoid. The Greek gods did not want to be bothered or moved by human passions or feelings. They did not want to risk loving fragile creatures. The gods did not want to subsume fragility into the makeup of what it meant to be divine.

Not Jesus. He was "deeply moved" by that which was deeply moving the people. Jesus was "greatly troubled" by that which was greatly troubling the people. Jesus allowed mortal feelings to disturb him. Jesus was not afraid to be stained by these human emotions. God entered into human suffering in the person of Jesus. Jesus was God's glass heart, sent into this world of trouble. And one can almost hear God's glass heart breaking as we read the short verse, "Jesus wept" (John 11:35). Jesus allowed himself to be overcome by human pain. He allowed his passion for us to break him.

Why did he do this? The Jews of the day knew the answer, "See how he loved him!" (John 11:36). The God of the Bible risked everything to experience this moment with humanity. God chose not to surround himself by the glories of heaven that he might surround himself by the graves of earth. Jesus wept because he loved; he loved Lazarus, Mary, and Martha.

You can substitute your name in that last thought: Jesus loves you. Jesus weeps for you and is "deeply moved" and "greatly troubled" over that which is afflicting you. Jesus weeps over that which you weep. If you ever wonder what God is doing when you have reached your limit, when you cannot move beyond tears, know that our God is weeping. He sees your pain and your tears and his heart shatters into a thousand

44

pieces. He weeps because he loves. "See how he loves you!"

He does not hold anything back from you. This is what is so attractive about Jesus Christ. He is fully human and fully divine. Though he has the power to help, as we will see in a moment, he also has the power to relate. God in Jesus can meet you wherever you are at, no matter how low or how lost. God can get there. Jesus can go into every dark corner, having the power to find you and the power to fix you. That is what it means to be fully human and fully God.

Ultimately, it means that God in Jesus is capable of having a relationship with you. God is not too big for you. God is not inaccessible from you. In the person of Jesus, God's world and your world meet. Just as in the one person of Jesus the worlds of divinity and humanity can meet, so can they meet in you. God can know you; you can know God. God can give his heart away to you; you can give your heart away to God. Jesus holds these worlds together, even through tears.

The Dimensions of God's Love

A pastor once told me that there are three kinds of people: someone who is in a storm, someone who is coming out of a storm, and someone who is headed back into a storm. His point was clear: life is full of storms. The skies will turn black and the clouds will dump down on your life. Lighting will strike and the wind will rage. What is going to hold it all together for you? You need a God who is not only bigger than the storm, but also a God who is in the storm with you. Jesus is both.

In the midst of the storm, Jesus unleashes a hurricane of his own. It is the hurricane of God's love. There is no situation or person that God's love cannot reach. Nothing can separate us from God's love. Consider these verses from the Apostle Paul:

And I pray that Christ will be more and more at home in your hearts as you trust in him. May your roots go down

45

deep into the soil of God's marvelous love. And may you have the power to understand, as all God's people should, how wide, how long, how high, and how deep his love really is. May you experience the love of Christ, though it is so great you will never fully understand it. Then you will be filled with the fullness of life and power that comes from God.
~ *Ephesians 3:17-19 (New Living Translation)*

God's love is wide and long and high and deep. In other words, it is all consuming. It is everywhere. You cannot escape it. It does not keep to itself, but is constantly reaching out to us. It reaches wide, it reaches long, it reaches high, and it reaches deep. It is going after people like us. It is going down to the depths to scrape off those who lay there. It is going to the ends of the earth to fetch those who are running from God.

Yet God's love "is so great you will never fully understand it." You will be lost in it like a drop is lost in the ocean. The more you know, the more it grows. It is, at the same time, a foundation beneath your feet and a shelter above your head. God's love is the power you need to get through the storm. Know that at any moment, God's powerful love is reaching out for you.

You will never be emotionally or spiritually mature if you are apart from God's love. Your roots need to grow down deeply into God's love. God's love needs to be the soil of your life. It holds you up and nourishes your existence. It surrounds you, protects you, and provides for you. Your growth will be stunted if you do not sink your roots deeply into God's love.

The Lord's Table

We see a vivid illustration of God's love when we consider what Christians call "the Lord's Table." Though Christians have had different understandings on the exact meaning of the Lord's Table over the centuries, all will agree on this: the Lord is the host. Let's consider what that means.

We know what it is like to be the host. When we have people over to our home, we are the host and they are the guests. As the host, our job is to serve the guest. We provide the meal; we buy it, bake it, and serve it. We keep plates full and glasses filled. We go back and forth from the kitchen to the dining room table, making sure the meal is running smoothly. As the host, it is our job to provide, from "soup to nuts."

We know what it is like to be served at a restaurant. After we order the meal, the waiter or waitress brings it to us. However, despite being taken care of so well, in the end, there is "no free meal." In the end, we have to pay. And in most cases, we even have to give the waiter or waitress extra money in the form of a tip.

We know what it is like to attend a potluck. At a potluck, we are supposed to bring a portion of the meal. Several people join together and each contributes to some part of the meal, whether the main dish, a side dish, a dessert, or a drink. Even though we get to eat the food that someone else brought, someone else gets to eat the food you brought!

Whether at home, a restaurant, or a potluck, one similarity is clear: the participants do the work. The participants pay or contribute in some way. But this is not the case with the Lord's Table. At the Lord's Table, the Lord is the Host. The Lord is the One who pays. The Lord is the One who provides the meal. At the Lord's Table, God does all the work. He says to the participants, "Sit down and eat."

Most of us are uncomfortable with this. We want to contribute in some way to this meal where salvation is served. We want to be the host. We want to put our good works on the table and draw attention to them. We come to the table with our public, decorated self, as if we earned our spot in God's dining room. We love to show off aspects of our faith performance. We love to point out all the reasons we should be there. We love to convince others that we contributed to the meal in some way. But the Lord of the Table says to us, "Sit down!"

47

"But, God, don't you want to see how much I love you?"

The Lord says, "Sit down." He continues, "Let me show you how much I love you."

Still, another person, who is sick from sin and feeble from failure, does not even approach the table. He stands at a distance, feeling totally unwelcome. He does not have the spiritual pedigree as others do. He has not had the same faith experiences. Her life is cracked like a broken mirror. Her life seems to be tied to a noose of bad choices. Yet the Lord says to the one who stands at a distance from his table, "Sit down."

"Lord, I don't deserve to be there with you."

"Sit down, my child. I want to be with you."

At the Lord's Table, the call is clear, "Sit down and let me be the Host. You are my beloved guest." God is the Provider, the Host, and the one who serves. God does the work before the meal and during the meal; he even cleans up afterward. God performs every role at the Table that serves salvation for its meal.

May you hear God's firm but gentle voice say to you, "Sit down and let me love you." We do not come to God standing as hosts, but kneeling as beggars for bread. He stands as your Host and Provider. You sit as his beloved. He serves his heart of love to you. Its dimensions surround you. At the table, his love is high and wide and long and deep. This is the third reason why you must not give up: you are loved by the Host. God has invited you to this world so that you could be served by him and discover his unconditional love for you.

You are here in this place to be loved. Ask God to show you his great love for you. Beg him to serve you. Sit and wait for his perfect meal; he will give you his heart.

Reason #4:

SOMEONE IS STANDING UP FOR YOU

She turned around and saw Jesus standing. ~ John 20:14

Jesus came and stood among them. ~ John 20:19 & 26

Jesus stood on the shore. ~ John 21:4

Stuck

The front man of U2 wrote a song about the suicide of his friend Michael Hutchence, the lead singer of the band INXS. The song is called *Stuck in a Moment You Can't Get Out Of.* The refrain of the song is, "You've got to get yourself together, you've got stuck in a moment and you can't get out of it. Oh love, look at you now! You've got yourself stuck in a moment and you can't get out of it." These words describe the atmosphere in which some of us live. Some of us are "stuck in a moment." No matter how hard we struggle, we just cannot seem to pry ourselves out. The moment overwhelms us and pulls us back to it again and again; it keeps us from moving on, from seeing hope, from being free. We are paralyzed.

This song can be sung not only to an individual, but also to the human race. The human race is "stuck in a moment."

49

The human condition is not free, no matter how often we like to tell ourselves we are. We are stuck in the condition of loss. We face the loss of the material, the spiritual, and the relational. We aim at life, but come up short, again and again. Loss is the air we breathe. For every victory, there is a loss. And it seems the losses last a lot longer. Yes, the flower blooms and we can enjoy it for a moment, but it soon fades and is gone forever. Loss is our universal human currency; and everything is being exchanged into loss. No wonder we get stuck in a moment. Perhaps our heart knows better than our head: nothing will stay. Our moments of grief are not really "moments" at all—they are what is and what will be. Tears are a sign that we are finally grasping the truth of the human condition.

We Are Mary

All of this comes together as we consider the activity, location, and posture of Mary in John 20. "But Mary stood weeping outside the tomb" (John 20:11). This small verse is a window into the human condition, allowing us to see how we are like Mary.

First, notice the activity. Mary is weeping. Mary is "stuck in a moment," which is more than a moment. Whether she realizes it or not, her weeping is not alone. Her tears are the drops that build a greater river. This river of loss has been building and raging for millennia. It is filled by the water in human faces. It is not fresh water, but bitter—as bitter as our salty tears. Mary's weeping is yet another stream that builds the ocean of grief, which is intrinsic to the human condition. We have cried like Mary for centuries, especially when death overthrows life.

Second, notice the location. Mary is outside of the tomb. She goes to the source of her pain. She wants to be with the one she cannot be with, which well summarizes the desperation of the human condition. Saint John, however, wants his

50

readers to see something else. We are to see the juxtaposition of Mary and the tomb. We are to see that for Mary, hope is dead. Hope is not with Mary, for that is why she weeps. Hope is in the tomb, dead and gone. Mary stands graveside of hope, as its chief mourner.

Third, notice the posture. Mary stands. This is John's subtle way of setting up the rest of this resurrection account. With this word "stand," a great contest is set into motion. On the one hand, you have the human condition. As we learned, it is our condition of loss. We weep, fear, and doubt, mourning the loss of hope and lacking faith. We are stuck in moment that we can't get out of. That is where we stand in one dark corner of the ring. But there is another corner, where Someone else stands. By noting the posture of Mary, we are encouraged to see the posture of Jesus. Mary is not the only one who stands. Jesus stands, too.

"But Mary stood weeping outside the tomb." This little verse provides vast insight into the great contest between the dismal human condition and the power of God. It captures our moment, on the one hand, yet it puts us into the greater moment that is unfolding, on the other. It is the moment when hope stood up.

Stand-Up

The Greek word "resurrection" literally means "stand-up." It's the word *anastasis*, from which the female name Anastasia and the male name Anastasios derive. *Ana* is a prefix meaning "up." The word *stasis* means "stand." The Resurrection is the event where Jesus stood up. There is no more powerful of a way to think about The Resurrection of Jesus Christ. The Resurrection is the event where one man finally stood up.

Saint John wants to make this point very clear to us. The careful reader will notice how John postures Jesus in each of The Resurrection appearances of John 20. In each appearance, John is careful to mention that Jesus was standing. Jesus is standing before Mary (John 20:14); the disciples, minus Thomas (20:19); and the disciples, including Thomas (20:26). (We will learn more about Thomas in chapter 7.)

Think of it simply like this: Jesus Christ was annihilated by torture and death on the cross at the hands of the Roman military; and Jesus stood up. It is as simple and spectacular as that. Jesus was crucified; Jesus had a spear thrust through his side to ensure his death; Jesus was wrapped in grave clothes; Jesus was placed in a known, secured tomb. Jesus stood up.

The Resurrection was the event where death took life to the mat in the ultimate grappling match, but after three days, only life stood up in victory. Death descended onto Jesus. Everyone assumed that death had won, for that is all the world has ever known. Nobody had ever beaten death. There was a chilling silence for three days. Then out of the dust, only One emerged. Only Jesus stood up in the end. Death had been defeated.

Seen like this, The Resurrection is the ultimate display of rebellion and power. Death stripped Jesus of his life and pinned him to the ground. But Jesus said in rebellion, "No!" And he stood up. Jesus was sick and tired of death having the last laugh. He was not going to put up with death anymore. It was finally time that somebody stood up to this ancient bully, a bully who has been stealing life from humanity since the beginning. The Resurrection is the greatest act of rebellion the world has ever known.

Think about this. No one showed more power than Jesus during that awful week. Sure, the authorities arrested Jesus and put him on trial, stripping him of his rights and dignity. Sure, they scourged him with a cat-of-nine-tails, opening his sides and breaking his ribs. Sure, they drove iron spikes into his hands and feet, crushing his bones. Sure, they rammed a spear into his side, puncturing his lungs and heart. Sure, the earth quaked and the sky turned black. Sure, there was intense sorrow and horrifying fear and relentless unbelief. But none of these did more damage than the single, defiant, rebellious act of Jesus standing up. When Jesus stood up he did more damage to suffering and evil than suffering and evil have ever done to us. When Jesus stood up, he killed that which was killing us. When Jesus stood up, he announced the death of death.

Or think about this from the disciples' point of view. They had no hope. Their hope was dead, literally. They were weeping graveside of it. They were scared. After all, they saw what happened to Jesus. They saw the harsh beatings and the crucifixion. They saw his lifeless body being taken down from the cross. They saw him being buried. They saw the Roman guard standing by the formidable tomb. They saw it all. And now he is back? What kind of man is this? What power he must have! This man is standing? An animal that has been slaughtered is not supposed to be standing—neither is a man who has been crucified. This is not supposed to be happening! No wonder the disciples were changed. The power of the resurrection would soon spring them from the conditions in which they were trapped, as we will learn in future chapters.

Picture your struggles as bombs that are dropped from a plane. Only, these bombs are all dropped on Jesus. The bomb of broken relationships, of depression, of doubt, and of sexual impurity lands on him. The bomb of childlessness, death, and pride lands on him. The bomb of self-reliance. The bomb of fear. The bombs of family tension, stress, sickness, and loneliness land on him, and on, and on, and on it goes. Bomb, after bomb, after bomb, land on Jesus. Each struggle drops down and explodes on the Son of God, erupting into a mushroom cloud of destruction. After all of this, you think that God is finally dead. Then the smoke slowly clears, and from the rubble and chaos and hopelessness and despair, one Man stands up.

The power of his Resurrection is greater than the power

of our sin and evil. Though the bitterness of the human condition is great, his resurrection power is greater still.

He Stands for You

Steve, a teenage boy, was a Juvenile Offender in the Department of Corrections. Rich was a pastor who led Bible studies for the kids in the Corrections facility. One day Rich went in for his usual small group Bible study. Before he could see any of the kids, the department head, Bob, pulled Rich into a staff meeting. Bob told Rich that he could not talk with Steve today, since Steve was both suicidal and homicidal. Steve was locked in his room and no one was allowed to see him. Rich agreed and went and met with some of the other kids. As Rich was being escorted out by Bob, right as he was about to leave the building, Rich heard God say to him, "You've got to go see Steve." Rich turned to Bob, the one who had forbid him to see Steve, and said, "I've got to go see Steve." Bob said that he wouldn't argue with a man of God and let Rich go into Steve's room.

Bob locked the door behind Rich and there he stood, looking at Steve, who was facing the wall on the opposite side of the room. Rich didn't know what to say; he only knew that God wanted him there. Rich saw a piece of paper on Steve's bed and assumed it was a note from Steve's girlfriend. To break the ice, Rich picked it up and started to read it. He found out that it was really a suicide note.

Rich then asked Steve how he was going to do it. Steve showed him a butcher knife that he stole from the kitchen. Rich called out to Steve, saying, "Steve, that tears me apart, because I love you!" Steve lunged toward Rich, dropping the knife as he came. He grabbed hold of Rich and hugged him with all he had. Through tears, Steve said, "I can't remember when someone has told me that they loved me!" And that moment was the beginning of great healing for Steve.[1]

[1] Adapted from *The Youth Workers Guide to Helping Teenagers in Crisis* by Rich Van Pelt and Jim Hancock (Grand Rapids: Zondervan, 2005), 66-68.

And it was all because one man stood up for him. One man said, "No! I need to tell Steve how much I love him!" One man did not want to leave Steve alone, trapped in his room. One man broke through, so to speak, and let Steve know that he was standing for him. It makes all the difference in the world if someone stands up for you.

We are all Steve, locked in our conditions. We lock others out and we lock God out. We feel trapped and do not want to go on living. But suddenly, Jesus appears, though the doors are locked. He stands up in front of us and holds out his scarred hand to us. He cries out, "This tears me apart, because I love you!"

He stands up against our human condition of loss and says, "No More!" Never has the world heard such a passionate declaration of fidelity. Never has the world had such a solid hope - one that stands no matter what. Though all hell breaks loose on your life, Jesus still stands. Nothing can keep his love away from you. Saint Paul puts it this way,

For I am sure that neither death nor life, nor angels nor rulers, nor things present nor things to come, nor powers, nor height nor depth, nor anything else in all creation, will be able to separate us from the love of God in Christ Jesus our Lord. - Romans 8:38-39

Picture a landscape that has been desolated by fire. Everything is smoldering. Everything has been destroyed. The land is black and hopeless. It seems that it is irrecoverable. Then one day, a single piece of green grass stands up. Against the ebony backdrop, one single life emerges from the rubble. One single piece of grass stands up in defiant rebellion against the fire that raged before it. Think about that field. Is that field hopeless? Should that field be condemned? The answer is no. So long as one piece of grass stands, there is hope. There can be vibrant life once again. Death has not had the last laugh.

Your life, no matter how black and smoldering, is not without hope, so long as one Man stands for you. Has everyone else left? Have you lost the things or people that were closest to you? Have you never known stability or life or joy? Do you feel like that hopeless, scorched field? Against the worst backdrop that you can paint, one Person stands for you. He will not sit down. He will not be beaten. He will not leave you. He stands always for you. On the brutal horizon of your life, know that at every moment, Someone is standing up for you.

That truth alone can keep you from taking your life today. All is not lost. Someone is standing for you, right now at this moment. As he stands, he is crying out to you, "This tears me apart, because I love you!"

The Auction

Let's imagine an auction. Only instead of bidding for cars or cabinets, we are bidding for people. In particular, you are on the auction block. In some ways, this is our "worst nightmare." We think about how it would be on the auction block, if the world had a chance to bid on us. Our worst nightmare is standing before silent bidders. We want people to bid on us. This scenario gets at the core of our human desire for love and acceptance. We want someone to spend big because they think we are worth it. They give us our worth, we feel, based on how much they are willing to give. "I am really worth something if someone gives up a lot to get me."

So put yourself on the auction block for a moment. There you are, standing vulnerable before the crowd of bidders. The auctioneer begins the bidding. He says something like; "I've got Sam here on the auction block. Sam Kee here. Who will give me $100 for Sam—any takers?" Then imagine an ensuing silence where nobody says a word. Nobody even

56

flinches. Silence. Nobody is willing to part with a mere $100 to bring Sam home. That is our worst nightmare!

Now let's replay the scene. For the sake of the illustration, let's put myself back on the auction block. There I stand before the bidders, vulnerable and aching for someone to give me my worth. The auctioneer begins the bidding. He says, "I've got Sam here on the auction block. Sam Kee, here. Who will give me $100 for Sam—any..."

Then before he can finish that sentence, a man in the back row flings up his hand with excitement. The man stands up. He rushes forward toward the auction block, shouting as he comes, "I'll take Sam! I'll take him! I'll give you my one and only son for him. I'll shed my son's blood right here on the auction block, if that's what it takes to get Sam for myself!"

There's an awkward silence and everyone is utterly stunned. The auctioneer tries to gain composure. He scrambles for his microphone. Stammering, the auctioneer says, "Man, don't go crazy on me, I only asked for 100 bucks."

The crazy man starts in, breathless and with passion in his eyes, "I don't care if it sounds crazy! I've got to have Sam. I've got to have him because I love him. I've got to have him back. I'll do whatever it takes to bring him home! I don't care how crazy it sounds."

The Simple Truth

The simple truth is that there is a God out there who is absolutely crazy for you. He is crazy enough to kill his one and only Son to get you back. He is crazy enough to kill his Son on a Roman cross, shedding his blood to pay the price for you. That is what God did for you on the auction block. He gave it all away for you to have you in his family. God is passionately in love with you. He is holding out his glass heart to you, realizing that it might shatter in the process of redeeming you.

When you are at your absolute worst, I want you to see

your crazy God, standing before you, willing to give it all to be with you. You are never without hope because you are never without love. Hope stands in your life, whether you know it or not. Hope stands up and makes a declaration of love for you. And hope will never fall to the ground, no matter how bad life gets. See hope standing at the auction block of your life, bidding it all to have you, giving it all to show you that you are worth it.

Your worth does not come from what you have lost in this life. Your worth comes from the price that God was willing to give for you. This is the fourth reason why you must not give up: Someone is standing up for you.

Reason #5:

You Are Released from Sorrow

But Mary stood weeping outside the tomb, and as she wept she stooped to look into the tomb. And she saw two angels in white, sitting where the body of Jesus had lain, one at the head and one at the feet. They said to her, "Woman, why are you weeping?" She said to them, "They have taken away my Lord, and I do not know where they have laid him." Having said this, she turned around and saw Jesus standing, but she did not know that it was Jesus. Jesus said to her, "Woman, why are you weeping? Whom are you seeking?" Supposing him to be the gardener, she said to him, "Sir, if you have carried him away, tell me where you have laid him, and I will take him away." Jesus said to her, "Mary." She turned and said to him in Aramaic, "Rabboni!" (Which means Teacher). Jesus said to her, "Do not cling to me, for I have not yet ascended to the Father; but go to my brothers and say to them, 'I am ascending to my Father and your Father, to my God and your God.'" Mary Magdalene went and announced to the disciples, "I have seen the Lord"—and that he had said these things to her.
~ John 20:11-18

59

Come on, oh my star is fading
And I see no chance of release
And I know I'm dead on the surface
But I'm screaming underneath

~ *Amsterdam* by Coldplay

Mary

While the band Coldplay did not write the song *Amsterdam* about Mary Magdalene, she could have sung it as her own nearly two thousand years before. Mary Magdalene had a rough life, to say the least. Saint Luke, the doctor, informs his readers that she once was inhabited by seven demons (Luke 8:3). She was a wealthy woman, but a hurting woman. Whether or not she was really inhabited by seven demons is not the point. Since seven was the number of "completion" for the ancients, Luke's point was to confirm to his readers that Mary was completely messed up. There was no hope for Mary, as the demons had total control of her life.

But then along comes Jesus. Jesus did not shun her because Evil had a hold of her. Jesus did not walk the other way when he saw her coming. He did the opposite: he went to her. He did more than just sympathize with her plight, though that would have been more than others had done. He healed her. He released her from the cage of demons and set her free—probably, for the first time in decades. So Mary moved from being a perfectly possessed person on the fringes of society to someone who was loved and surrounded by the community of Jesus. He welcomed her into his family of followers. She suddenly had new friends and a new found purpose. She got her mind back and her life back. Life was finally going well for Mary.

60

Then they killed him. The authorities killed the first person that finally accepted Mary. They took the life of the One who gave Mary life. The first person that finally did something decent for Mary was gone, and she cannot even find his body to give him a proper burial. First she lost his life, and now, she lost his body! Her whole world was stripped away in just one weekend. She had no closure and did not know where to turn. No wonder Mary was a mess, no wonder she wept, and no wonder she could not move on from the tomb.

Dead on the Surface

As in *Amsterdam*, Mary could not release herself from the grip of the tomb. She could not pry herself from her sorrow. She was "dead on the surface," but she was "screaming underneath." The other two disciples came to the tomb and left, but not Mary. Though Peter and John depart, Mary remains. She comes out from the shadows, weeping. She is a woman who has been chained to the night and there is no mention of the dawn from Saint John the writer. As readers, so far, we are in the dark place with Mary. It is still night for us, too. If you were reading John's book for the first time, you would be on the same page with Mary, needing resolution. Your tears would trap you, too. Where was Jesus? Where did his body go? "Where was the man who gave me the only unconditional love I have ever known?" Neither you nor Mary would be able to release yourself from the iron bars of grief. Mary did not weep passively. Neither would you.

Have you ever been stuck in a mood? No matter how hard you tried, you just could not pull yourself out of it? You tried to find release, but you could not find it. Everything was still dark. There was nothing but a vacant hole in the ground. Your friends gave up and left. There you are, like Mary, dead on the surface, but screaming underneath. You have the will to be released, but not the power. Neither do you have the freedom to be released. The cage is on top of you; the quicksand is beneath you. You are stuck. And the more you cry, the wetter the earth becomes, holding your feet all the more in the mud. You are screaming underneath. Though you do not weep passively, nobody hears and nobody seems to understand. You just get question after question, as did Mary from the angels, as if something were wrong with you and not the situation.

That was Mary's world, as she peered inside the tomb and saw the two angels sitting where the body of Jesus had been. On the one hand, this shows how far gone Mary really was. For there were two angelic beings right in front of her, but this did not faze her. She was so trapped by sorrow that she still could not see the fingerprints of God. The angels were right in front of her face, but her face could only see the cloud of sorrow before her eyes. She was blinded from seeing the hand of God. She was so sunk in the mud, that even two angels did not fathom her.

"Woman, why are you weeping?" was their question to Mary. Grief is like that. To outsiders, the angels, our grief does not always make sense. But to the one trapped within the grief, our tears make perfect sense, "They have taken away my Lord, and I do not know where they have laid him" (20:13). Her life is missing. Her hope is gone. "Not only has hope been taken away, but also I do not even know where to look next." You can feel Mary's loneliness and desperation. Though you plop two angels right before her eyes, it does not scratch the surface of her grief. She is completely dead on the surface. The reader is left wondering, "What can possibly spring Mary from this cage of mourning?" Can anything get her out?

The Valley of Vision

The only other time that Saint John mentions angels is in the first chapter of his book. Jesus says to one of his followers,

Truly, truly, I say to you, you will see heaven opened, and the angels of God ascending and descending on the Son of Man. *~ John 1:51*

In the empty tomb, the angels had descended "on the Son of Man." At least, they were stationed where the Son of Man had been laid. One angel was at the head; the other was at the foot. They encompassed the spot where his body had been. It is as if God is saying to Mary, "The heavens are opened right now to you, Mary. The angels have descended and are surrounding the thing that is causing you grief." When we are grieving, there is a moment when we gain vision. God will grant us vision in the midst of our suffering that others will not have. The Puritans called this "the valley of vision." It is the dark valley in which we walk where we can see the light of God more clearly than if we were not in the valley.

Mary is in the dark valley and the heavens are opened for a moment. She receives a vision from God. God surrounds her grief, just as the angels surround the spot where Jesus had been. Even though Mary feels so trapped and alone, God is beginning to penetrate her world. All hope is not gone. A hole in the wall of grief has been bored—a portal through which God is beginning to enter.

When you are trapped by sorrow, look for the hand of God. God will not always give you instant release, but he will send hope just when you need it. He will not release you completely, all at once. But he will enter your sorrow and sit quietly with you, like the unassuming angels in the tomb. God will give you a little glimpse of light, shining into your cave, just when you need it. Don't miss it. See God surrounding your situation, as angels surrounded Mary's situation. Though she did not recognize the hand of God at first, God was still there. Though you might not recognize the hand of God at work in your valley, God is still there. My prayer for you is that he would turn your dark, clouded valley into a valley of vision.

The Boy in the Pit

There was once a boy who had suffered a great deal in his life. One day, he found himself being lowered by a single rope down into a dark pit. He was being lowered down toward the bottom very slowly. He did not know how he got on the end of this rope or who held the other end. He did not know why he was being lowered into a pit, either. He just knew that he was descending deeper and deeper into the darkness.

He tried to call out for help, but nobody answered. He called out to God, but God did not come to his rescue. The boy strained his neck looking upward to the surface. He kept looking toward the fading light above him, calling out to God with desperate cries. "God, help me!" and "God, save me!" But there was no answer. He kept looking upward toward God, but God did not help him.

The boy finally hit the bottom of the pit. It was dark and terrifying. The boy did not want to give up, so he kept looking for a rescuer to come. He kept straining his neck by looking upward toward the miniscule sky, now barely visible. Minutes passed and still no answer. After hours passed, the boy lost hope. He slowly lowered his head in defeat. As he lowered his head, he saw something that he could not believe, right in front of him on the ground in the pit. There on the ground before him was God, with arms outstretched, waiting for him. The boy was finally low enough to see God.

When you are in the dark pit, God probably will not come from above. God will probably be in the pit with you, waiting for you to notice. God does not rescue from without, but from within. God enters our dark world with us in order to deliver us. He is at the bottom of our pain, not the top. He sits quietly like an angel, waiting for us to notice.

Broken Mirrors

I sat and listened as Katie poured out her heart out to me,

64

telling me about her childhood. Her biological father was abusive and eventually her parents divorced. But Katie had to stay with her father, because her mom did not want her. Her dad eventually married again and then got another divorce. Then he decided that he did not want her, either. So Katie was adopted by her step-mom, from her dad's second failed marriage, since neither of her biological parents wanted her.

All of Katie's life had been a fight. She had low self-esteem. She thought that she was ugly, though she was not. She thought that she was dumb, though she was not. She thought that she was unlovable, though she was not. Suffering found her wherever she went. She was abused physically, sexually, and emotionally; she was abandoned and she was broken.

Broken. That word stood out to me as I listened to Katie. Then God put a thought in my mind.

"Katie," I said to her. "It seems to me that you have been surrounded by broken mirrors your whole life." She waited to hear more. "We look into mirrors to see who we are," I continued. "But you are surrounded by broken mirrors. These mirrors are broken people and experiences and hurtful actions that reflect back to you a poor image. When you look into the mirror of your parents, you get a broken reflection, since they are broken. Every mirror in your life is broken. And you cannot see who you really are. All you see is the person reflected out of their brokenness. And that's not who Katie really is. You need to find a mirror that is not broken. Then you will see who you truly are."

A strange thing happens to us when we suffer. If we suffer long enough and hard enough, the pain becomes a part of our identity. The brokenness we experience turns into the broken person we see in the mirror. Pain becomes the person. Instead of merely having problems, we feel that we are the problem. Katie did not just have bad parents; she felt that she was bad. She began to make huge identity statements about herself. "I am unlovable." "I am unwanted." "I am the prob-lem." She could not define herself outside of the evil things done to her. Not only were her clothes wet with suffering, but also was her soul.

When we look into broken mirrors, we see a broken per-son staring back at us. And if a broken mirror is the only one we have, then we begin to think that we really are broken. "It's not just the mirror, it's me!" we believe. Our identity shifts and we no longer say, "I am loved," or "I am smart," or even, "I am Katie." We say much worse things. We say broken things. We say awful things. We turn ourselves into monsters. "I am pathetic." "I am an idiot." "I am worthless."

When all we see is brokenness, after a while, we turn into a "problem" rather than a person. What do you do with a problem? You destroy it.

Those are the thoughts that Katie, Mary, and perhaps you have experienced. But remember, you need another mir-ror. You need a mirror that is not broken. You cannot make an accurate identity statement about yourself when you only gaze into a broken mirror. You need a solid mirror to find out the truth; to see who you really are.

Shepherd

I told Katie that she needed an unbroken mirror to see who she really was. She was neither a problem nor unwanted, she was Katie, plain and simple. She was loved by God. If anyone ever asked her the question, "Who are you?" I told her the answer. "Katie, you are loved." That is who you are. When you look at God, he reflects back his unbroken love for you. He loves perfectly because he is perfect.

It is remarkable to see how Jesus approaches Mary in the garden outside of the tomb. Up to this point, nothing has been able to release her from her sorrow. Sorrow had its grip on her, such that it went deeper than the moment. Sorrow had been with Mary her whole life. Her identity had no doubt been conformed to its image. Though Jesus had given her a couple of good years of relief, it did not take much to fling her back into her old ways. Having seven demons, as we learned, would cause one to be an emotional, social, and physical outcast. All three of these have surfaced once again. She is back in the rut. You can see her identity cracking and crumbling as the story unfolds. You feel sorry for Mary. She is not shaken by the report of the two disciples, she does not respond to the presence of the two angels, and she does not flinch at the sight of Jesus himself, when she mistakes him for the gardener. The old, broken Mary is back. What can release her from this dangerous existence?

Jesus stands up in her emotional prison and calls out her name. "Mary!" Jesus says (20:16). Jesus is as tender as a shepherd with his trembling sheep. One cannot help but think of Jesus' words earlier in Saint John's story,

I am the good shepherd. I know my own and my own know me. The sheep hear his voice, and he calls his own sheep by name and leads them out. ~ *John 10:14 and 10:3*

In the first moment of clarity for Mary, Jesus calls her by name. "Mary!" It is as if he holds a mirror up to her face and gives her back herself. "Mary!" Only Jesus is the mirror. As she looks into his perfect image, she finally sees herself and is led out of her sorrow. "He calls his own sheep by name and leads them out."

For the ancients, to give a name was to give an identity. Names were more than just ways of keeping track of many people. Your name represented your identity. It went more than skin deep. Recall how Jesus gave one of his disciples the name "Peter," for Jesus was looking for a "Rock" on which to build his church (Matthew 16:18). "Peter" was more than a name; it was an identity and calling. One cannot help but wonder what Mary heard when Jesus identified her as "Mary." It had to go deeper than surface level. For this was the event that finally catapulted Mary from her sorrow. Not only did Mary recognize Jesus, but also she recognized herself. After all, in response to his call, she does not say, "Jesus!" Instead, she says, "Rabboni!" or "Teacher!" This was Jesus' best lesson to her. He taught her who she was. She was not hopeless. She was not the woman with seven demons. She was Mary. It took his unbroken face to convince her of it. This sheep heard the shepherd's voice when he called her by name. Then he led her out. He led her out of her sorrow.

Perfect People Perfect People

So God's glass heart turns out to be a mirror. I will never forget some words from my mentor many years ago, when I was just starting out in ministry. He said to me, "Hurt people hurt people." That lesson has never left me. Broken people break people. When someone does something rotten to you, you can be almost certain that someone else had done something rotten to him first.

But if "hurt people hurt people," then it also could be said, "perfect people perfect people." If hurt people hurt out of their brokenness, then perfect people perfect out of their wholeness. We all know that no one but One is perfect. You and I and our neighbors are not perfect. Mary was not perfect. Jesus was the only perfect person. Thus, he is the only one who can make us perfect. Perfect people perfect people.

He is the only perfect mirror. He is the only one who can show us who we were meant to be, before the human condition marred the image of God on our faces. By staring into his perfect being, we see our potential. Our shattered lives come together. We see that we are not broken so long as we view ourselves through Jesus' eyes. We are both healed and being healed. Life comes together in the face of Jesus, who is God.

As God, Jesus has the ability to rescue and restore. Jesus gives us a new Genesis, as we become his new creation. Once we were created in God's image and once we were shattered by Adam's image. Finally, in Jesus, our broken lives are restored.

You may think that this is all pie-in-the-sky. You may think that I am going overboard, going to where Scripture does not go. After all, Jesus merely spoke Mary's name; surely he did not remake her, give her a new identity, and perfect her all at once, as was said. If this all seems too strange or too good to be true, then please consider the words of Saint Paul to the Corinthians. Right at the point where Paul refers to people as broken, clay vessels, he proclaims all of what I said with just one verse.

For God, who said, "Let light shine out of darkness," has shone in our hearts to give the light of the knowledge of the glory of God in the face of Jesus Christ.
~ 2 Corinthians 4:6

When God said, "Let light shine out of darkness," he was creating the world in the beginning. When we see the face of Jesus Christ, we gain the same kind of Genesis light. The light we see in the face of Jesus is light that can make us new once again. It is light that has the power to heal our brokenness. It is light that can spring us from chaos, darkness, and depth. For this light plunges us in the ocean of God's glory. And when we see God's glory, we are set free from human depravity. In short, we are born again.

When God spoke in Genesis 1:1, light came into the darkness. When Saint John began his account of Jesus, he began with this same powerful speech into the darkness, "In the beginning was the Word, and the Word was with God, and the Word was God... The light shines in the darkness, and the darkness has not overcome it" (John 1:1, 5). When Jesus spoke the name "Mary," light came into the darkness that shrouded the tomb. Life came from the voice of the "Gardener." Just as God spoke the world into being in Genesis, God speaks our being into the world in John. The shepherd's voice gives new life. God makes us whole again.

The academics tend to pick on John Calvin for his negative statements about human beings. Calvin had a habit of dehumanizing those who do not love God. Calvin, however, follows the ancient Christian thinker Augustine in this matter. Both of these men believed that humans were never meant to be separated from God. If a person is separated from God, then that person is less than she was created to be. If a person is not united with Jesus Christ, then he falls short of being fully human, as God intended. You are only whole when you are wholly God's. God makes us complete. God heals our shattered lives.

Making It Personal

It was as if Mary were in an emotional catatonic state. Nothing budged her. She was so steeped in sorrow that little was able to shake her out of it. Though the tomb was empty, she still wept. Though two angels spoke to her, she still cried. Though she spoke to Jesus himself, she was still gripped by sorrow. The person she grieved for was right there in front of her and she missed him completely. That is how bad her pain was, on the one hand. That is how possible it is to miss Jesus, though he is right in front of you, on the other.

You can overlook Jesus though he is right in front of you. The man who loved her and died for her is standing up right in front of her—and she nearly missed him! What a tragedy it would have been if she lived-out the rest of her life assuming that the man in the garden on that morning was just the gardener. What a tragedy it would be if you lived the rest of your life thinking that Jesus was no more important than a common gardener. He could be calling your name right now and you could be missing it. You might think that Jesus is standing up for someone else; but he is standing up for you.

I remember the first time that it became personal for me. I had heard about Jesus as I was growing up. But he was no more important to my life than just another gardener—or construction worker or milkman or whatever. He was just a common man. There was nothing all that special about him and he did not hold a special place in my life. He held no more of a special place than the mechanic or grocery clerk. I just assumed that he was like everyone else. I did not think of God as being personal. He was in the background of my life, quietly pruning the shrubs and pulling the weeds.

When I was in college, it all changed. Suddenly, I heard his voice calling my name. Suddenly, the Gardener got personal. I realized for the first time that God wanted to have a personal relationship with me. I learned that God went to great lengths to win me back. I came to know that God became the person Jesus, who suffered excruciating pain in my place. Jesus was flogged with whips and rods for me. Jesus had nails driven into his hands and feet for me. Jesus was raised up on the cross for me. Jesus was pierced by a spear for me. Jesus could have stopped the spear, but instead, he chose to have it rammed into his side, tearing apart his lungs and bursting open his heart, for me. He did it for me. He was tortured for me. I was in his mind. Jesus did not come to die for the good people around me; he came for me specifically.

He wants me and he loves me. Saint Paul makes it incredibly personal too, when he writes these passionate words (notice the personal pronoun "me"):

The life I now live in the flesh I live by faith in the Son of God, who loved me and gave himself for me
~ Galatians 2:20

71

You have got to make it personal, too. You cannot go on living like God only cares for those other people. You cannot go on living like God is not crazy for you. God did not come for those other people—don't worry about them—God came for you. God loves you. God became a person so that each person could experience his intimate and personal love. God bled for you and suffered in your place. God wants to rescue you and, yes, God stands up for you. It is your name that he is calling out. Forget about "Mary," he is calling your name right now. Stop pretending that he is just the gardener. Stop living with God in the background, quietly maintaining your life so that things do not get too overgrown. Jesus is not just the gardener; he is the lover of your soul. He is calling out your name. He came to the garden to rescue you.

The Romance

Saint John is subtly telling another kind of story. Not only is he telling us the story of Mary's rescue from sorrow, but also he is telling us the story of Mary and the Lover of her soul. The Bible's Old Testament has a book called The Song of Songs, which is a great love story, telling of a man pursuing a woman in a garden. The story is filled with romance and fragrance. One cannot help but see the same story unfolding here. Mary is being pursued by a man in a different garden that is filled with spices from the burial. Only this man will not "love her and leave her." Jesus offers her perfect love and is the perfect Husband. He calls out her name and she rushes to embrace him.

In fact, she holds so tightly onto him, that he has to tell her, "Do not cling to me" (20:17). Mary lost him once; she sure does not want to lose him again. He is the man she has been looking for her whole life, the One that she was made for. He had her name on his lips.

Jesus is the One that you were made for, too. Your name

is on his lips and he is pursuing you in this garden of life. He wants to lavish personal love on you. Please do not ignore him when he calls your name. Remember, it is you that he is after. He calls you by name so that when you hear his voice, he can lead you out. He can lead you out of your cage of sorrow. When he stood up, he burst a hole right through it.

From Mourning to Mission

It is incredible to think that God would use Mary Magdalene as his first missionary. Think about Mary: she was scary, having had seven demons. No reasonable person would ever let her into his home, let alone grant her the solemn charge of being the first voice to utter the words that would change the globe for good: "He is risen!" God gave Mary the honor of being the first one to let the world know that its greatest enemy had been undone. There is simply no greater message to tell. God entrusted this message to a woman who once had seven demons possessing her and attacking her soul. Even more, she was totally incompetent due to the fact that she was paralyzed by sorrow. Her life was at a standstill. Who is to say that one more disappointment might not fling her back into her cage? Who is to say that the demons might not latch back onto her and cripple the spread of the good news?

Jesus chose Mary and changed her from a mourner to a missionary. God will often take the worst bits of us and change them into the best bits for others. Right at the spot where we suffer the worst, God is likely to spring us into mission. Our miseries travel the best when it comes to telling the good news of Jesus' stand. The very thing that we hate the most, God will employ. God released Mary from her sorrow only to send her ahead. She was not allowed to cling to him, though it is understandable why she wanted to do so, because she had a job to do. God loves to take our tears and turn them into service.

Know that God can take your affliction and redeem it.

Because Mary was stuck in the rut of mourning, she was in the right spot at the right time. Your tears are never lost, so listen for God to call your name. Our Good Shepherd will call your name and lead you out. When he leads you out, he will give you a sacred job to do. God does not lead you out of sorrow and leave you to face an empty calendar. God leads you out of sorrow and then fills your time with his kingdom's work. To keep you from drifting back toward the cage, he binds you to mission.

Expectations

Mary began her day before sunrise. Perhaps she could not sleep that night. The most significant person in her life was dead. She did not have much else to fall back on—a woman who arrives fresh from seven demons does not have much social capital to work with. She went to the tomb in order to care for Jesus' body and continue the grieving process. She never expected what she found—or did not find. She did not find Jesus' body. Neither could Peter or John find his body. They went home, but Mary stayed at the tomb, since she could not move on. A great emotional chain held her to the spot. A cage of grief descended upon her. She did not know where release might come from.

To be fair, Mary had the same expectations that we would have. When you go to a burial place, you expect to find the dead. She did not have the categories for anything else; neither would we. We go to funerals expecting to see the dead lying in a casket. We assume this, because that is all the world has ever known: the dead stay dead. We would not even think to imagine a funeral where our deceased loved one was walking around the funeral parlor with the rest of us. That is unimaginable. It is barely polite to write about that situation without being offensive. We go to funerals to mourn, not to play games by imagining standing corpses. That does not help anyone.

74

Mary expected what all humans expected after someone dies. You cannot blame her for not noticing the living Jesus. A living crucifiee is a foreign concept, never before introduced onto the human landscape. In fact, it presents new landscape altogether. A living crucifiee has never grown from the soil of this earth before. After all, from dirt we came and to dirt we shall return (Genesis 3:19). One gets the sense that perhaps Mary said more than she knew when she called him the "gardener." This standing gardener was bringing life where there was none. This gardener was replanting the Garden of Eden, starting with Jesus, on the first day of the week—which was also the first day of creation according to the Hebrew Bible. Jesus was the first plant to stand up in the garden, which feels an awful lot like a new Genesis rather than just the end of John.

The reader's expectations are tied with Mary's at this point. All at once, we come to the end of the story and the beginning of the story. We turn a corner. We change books. We are no longer trudging through the old book of the human condition, which has few happy scenes. We begin the first chapter of the new book of hope, where mourners show up to funerals only to find gardeners rather than corpses. This is something new. The Resurrection changes everything, whether you're ready or not.

The Resurrection has the power to release you from grief and spring you to mission. The Resurrection opens up possibilities that were not there before. The Resurrection restores our name; names that were once broken become whole. Though our world falls apart, it comes together when Jesus stands up for us. The stand releases us from the story of sorrow by introducing the story of love. You do not have to remain trapped in the pages of sorrow, now that there is a new chapter of hope.

Hear Jesus call your name for perhaps the first time. Know that it is you that he is coming after. He wants to lead you out. Someone else might have called you a failure. Someone else might have shattered your world with hurtful words or harmful actions. You may feel like it is impossible for you to move on in life. Jesus is standing before you with a new Genesis in mind. He will not tell you to give the old life a try one more time. He is not naive like that. He knows that the old ways will not work. He knows that you have been through unthinkable pain. Instead, he will point you to a new life with him. He will ask you to be born again. The fifth reason why you must not give up is that you are released from sorrow.

Reason #6:

You Are Released from Fear

On the evening of that day, the first day of the week, the doors being locked where the disciples were for fear of the Jews, Jesus came and stood among them and said to them, "Peace be with you." When he had said this, he showed them his hands and his side. Then the disciples were glad when they saw the Lord. Jesus said to them again, "Peace be with you. As the Father has sent me, even so I am sending you." And when he had said this, he breathed on them and said to them, "Receive the Holy Spirit. If you forgive the sins of any, they are forgiven them; if you withhold forgiveness from any, it is withheld."
~ John 20:19-23

Two Kinds of Fear

When I was a boy, I had two great fears. One was a fear of not being. The other was a fear of being. Let me explain.

First, I'll explain not being. I used to play an imagination game about death. I would play this game with all the mental abilities that I could muster. I would only do it a couple times a

77

year, because it was so terrifying to me. I would try to imagine what it would be like to be dead. But even as a boy I knew that the game itself lacked logical consistency, for if I could imagine what it would be like to be dead, then I would not be dead. Dead people do not imagine and they cannot wonder. Dead people cannot experience being dead, for there is no experience in death. Knowing this, I would imagine what it would be like not to imagine at all or "not to be." I tried to experience the non-experience. At this point in the "exercise" I would really start to scare myself. I would have to "pull out." It was always way too much for a boy to handle. I simply could not fathom there not being a "me" to process the world around me.

This was the fear of not being. It carried with it the assumption that there is no soul or life apart from the body. As a boy, I assumed that once my body stopped functioning physically, then I would cease to be once and for all. I did not know about the soul and did not think about an afterlife. This life was all there was—or so I thought. I feared the day when physical harm would be done to me such that my life would be taken away.

My second fear was that of being. Whereas my first fear had to do with the physical person of Sam, this second fear has to do with the identity of Sam. As a teenager, I would spend time in front of the mirror wondering about all the ways that I might fail in life. I would wonder who would ever accept or love me. I wondered if I would ever do anything noteworthy to help the world. I wondered how I might hurt other people, as I grew older. I wondered who this person in the mirror would become. I feared my own being. What if I messed up? What if I failed? Would anyone still love me? Would I go too far? Who was I? Would I become a good person or a bad person? How would it all turn out for that boy looking back at me in the mirror? This second fear, as I later realize, has to do with identity. Men, in particular, struggle with identity and failure.

We do not want to fail, because then we feel like we will not be anybody. We do not want our talents to be wasted, for then we will not be anybody. We want to be successful, for then we will be somebody special. We fear not being special, not being accepted, and not being loved.

It seems to me that all other fears can be categorized within these two kinds of fears: not being and being. On the one hand, there are many fears of not being. We fear death or anything else that threatens our security. We could list hundreds, if not thousands of fears that threaten us in this way, from spiders to airplanes to nuclear warfare. On the other hand, there are many fears of being. We fear the things that threaten our identity as a person, family, or community. We fear losing our good name or reputation. We fear not being accepted in a group. We fear doing something that will push us out of the reach of love. We fear what we might do as human beings. Again, hundreds if not thousands, of fears threaten us in this way.

I want you to think about your fears as you begin this chapter. Do you struggle with fears of not being or being? You probably struggle with both, as I do. Now, do not hear me wrongly, all fears are not bad. But let's face it, fears can be paralyzing when they get out of control. There are healthy fears, to be sure, but there are also fears that keep us locked in at night. We fear what might happen if we show ourselves to the world. Will they hate me? Will they kill me? I know that sounds dramatic, but fears bring drama into our lives. Fears often dramatize that which does not need to be. Some fears are rationale, but some are quite irrational.

The bottom line, nonetheless, is that fear can trap us just like sorrow. Mary needed to be released from sorrow. In this chapter, we will see that the disciples needed to be released from fear. The disciples had both kinds of fear, too, as we will see. We will also see how the resurrected Jesus released them from these fears, more accurately, how he empowered the disciples to face them. Ultimately, I want you to know that you do not have to remain paralyzed by your fears, so long as Jesus is standing for you.

The Mood

What are you afraid of? The dark? Snakes? Public speaking? Scary movies? Whatever it is that scares you, try to imagine the first disciples' world of fear at this moment. Saint John paints the mood well with his words. He starts by saying that it was in the evening—it was dark. So far in John's book, the "night" has not been good. John has been associating nighttime with evil. After all, when Judas left to commit the most hideous betrayal the world has ever known, John comments with these pithy words, "And it was night" (John 13:30). Evil lurks in the dark; hopelessness reigns at night. The night is full of threats. There are unseen enemies who will do you great harm. You had better stay indoors.

John also tells us that the doors were locked. That's how scared the disciples were. Not only were they hiding inside at night, but also they locked the doors. One does not lock the doors simply because he is afraid of the dark. One locks the doors when there are enemies outside. The disciples had enemies crouching at the door, so to speak, waiting to attack.

And just in case we have missed the intensity of the situation for the disciples, John flat out tells us that the disciples were hiding "for fear of the Jews" (John 20:19). There were certain Jewish people stalking about who, no doubt, sought to do the disciples great harm. If they killed their leader, Jesus, then they may kill his followers. The atmosphere is thick with fear.

My siblings and I had a Halloween party at our rural property when we were in high school. It was dark. We had a bonfire, dressed in frightening costumes, and told scary stories.

We even created a haunted walk through the woods for this perfect October night.

Then it happened. Then he came out of the woods. A man in mechanics coveralls stormed out of the woods. He wore a ski mask and bore a chainsaw. He began chasing teenagers around the yard, revving the chainsaw as he ran. It was dramatic. Kids were running and screaming for their lives. Everyone was terrified.

Though I knew that the man was my dad and though I knew that he took the chain off of the chainsaw, so it would be safe, I was still scared! Now just imagine if that scenario were real. It would be absolutely horrifying. It would be paralyzing. When a man is chasing you with a chainsaw, you cannot think of anything else. You do not worry about your wardrobe, your plans for Saturday night, or your favorite television show. You have only one paralyzing thought on your mind: how am I going to escape!

Faced with threats over their lives and drowned in an atmosphere of fear, the disciples were paralyzed. They locked themselves in, praying that their enemies would not find them. In order to understand what the disciples were going through, you have to place yourself in an atmosphere of fear. But maybe that is where you are at right now, fearing the enemies at your own door. You have locked yourself away because of fears that threaten your security or identity. You are paralyzed to think about much else. You cannot stop thinking about what might happen should you go outside. So you keep the doors locked.

We lock more than just physical doors. We lock emotional, intellectual, social, and spiritual doors. We face enemies in all of these areas. Enemies may be material or non-material. You can carry around your atmosphere of fear wherever you go, even outdoors. You may fear relationships because of how you have been hurt in the past. You may fear letting others have control, because if you are not in control, then things fall apart—at least they did at home with your alcoholic parent. You may fear opening your heart to God because of how someone in a church has hurt you or spoken ill of you. You are afraid to take the next step, because the next step hurt deeply in the past. It is safer just to stay locked emotionally away behind closed doors. At least then the man with the chainsaw cannot come in. We are like the child who pulls the blanket over his head so that the ghosts cannot touch him.

We Are Not Safe

But we are not safe. To be sure, we do a great job of keeping people at a distance. We lock ourselves away when we need to, so as to keep enemies at bay. We have learned to live in this atmosphere of fear, adjusting well to life behind locked doors, blankets, and menacing mechanics. But we are not safe and nor do we want to be. We want someone to find us. We hate living like this. If we are honest with ourselves, it is exhausting being constantly on watch. We have little energy left. We long to be released from this atmosphere of fear. We do not want to be paralyzed any longer. We want the freedom of walking outdoors beneath the clear sky once again; we want joy to dawn in our darkness.

The disciples were not safe. As they huddled together behind locked doors for fear of their Jewish enemies, Jesus breaks in. Saint John writes, "Jesus came and stood among them" (John 20:19). Though the doors were locked, Jesus came in anyway. The disciples were safe from everyone but him. Jesus pays no regard to our locks and chains. Our shelters cannot keep him out. Ready or not, here he is.

Imagine what that must have been like for the disciples. The last time they saw Jesus, blood was draining out of his mangled and lifeless body. Jesus was completely defeated. His body was bound up and he was discarded in a cave. Jesus was the last person on their minds. He was the last person in the world they expected to break down their walls. With their eyes on the enemy, little did they expect to see their friend standing. The moment must have been breathtaking. Like a thunderclap to rouse them from their paralyzed place, Jesus stood up in their midst. They did not believe Mary's report to them; this is demonstrated by the fact that they were still scared and behind locked doors. Sometimes the report from another is just not good enough. We need to see Jesus for ourselves. God needs to stand up in our situation to get our attention. To put it directly, when Jesus stood up in the middle of the room, he got their attention.

Nothing can keep Jesus away from you. Nothing. It may take a miracle for him to get in, but he will get in, I promise. Nothing can separate you from his love (remember Romans 8?). You are not "safe" from his love. His love can reach you. His love can stand up for you no matter how thick your walls may be, no matter how long you have been hiding there, and no matter how scary the threat at the door.

Earlier in John's book, we learn about the time when Jesus raised Lazarus from the dead. Lazarus was the brother of Mary and Martha (we learned about their situation in chapter three). When Lazarus came out of the grave, he was still bound by his grave clothes. Lazarus had to have others unbind them from his body. Contrast Lazarus with Jesus. When Jesus came out of the grave, he passed right through his grave clothes. In fact, as we learned in chapter two, he left the grave clothes behind, right in the spot where Jesus passed through them in the tomb. This shows a fundamental difference between Lazarus' resurrection and Jesus' Resurrection. Lazarus "rewound" his life, while Jesus undid his own death. Jesus passed through death. Lazarus did not pass through death, but merely backed up to an earlier moment in life. Nothing fundamental changed about Lazarus. He just "restarted." Jesus, on the other hand, was released.

Jesus also passed through the walls of the disciples' home. He probably passed through the walls the same way he passed through the grave clothes. However Jesus passed through, or with what kind of body he was raised with, does not matter. What matters is that he did it. Jesus passed through. He passed through death and rock and linen and plaster. And if he can pass through all of that, then he can pass through whatever wall you are trapped by. Jesus can penetrate into any situation you find yourself. You are never alone. You are never beyond his reach. You may feel all alone and you may feel like no one can rescue you, but that simply is not true. Jesus can stand in the darkest corner of the deepest fear. He can be by your side in less than a moment and stand with you for more than a millennia. Pray to him and ask him to come into your situation.

A Closer Look at Fear

What is fear? Fear is our response to a threat that might bring us harm in the future. Fear has a nervous eye to the future. Something dreadful is looming on the horizon. Fear detects the things that threaten our not being or being. We are afraid for our physical or mental safety.

Recall my two broad categories of fear earlier in this chapter, that of not being and being. The disciples were crippled by both, as we can see from John 20:19-23. It is obvious why they were crippled by the fear of not being. The Jewish authorities just murdered their leader. Surely the same authorities would hunt them next? They were far more vulnerable than Jesus. At least Jesus had throngs of supporters. If the authorities were willing to risk going against the enthusiasm of the multitude of Jesus' supporters, then obviously they would not hesitate to capture and kill his followers, who had little or no support. Nothing or nobody would stop eleven more crucifixions (the Twelve minus Judas Iscariot). The disciples were scared of physical death or not being.

84

Not only that, but they were also scared of being. Recall that the fear of being, as I defined it, has to do with a threat to one's identity. You live with the fear of being someone you despise. You fear what will become of your reputation, especially if you become a failure or laughingstock. You fear being known as one of the enemy. Think of the husband who would rather end his life than be known as a man without a successful career or faithfulness in his marriage. Think of the young lady who quietly cuts away at her life rather than being a daughter who cannot live up to her parents' high expectations. We will kill ourselves over an identity we either have not achieved (if it is positive) or have achieved (if it is negative). If you get labeled negatively as "worthless," then you might decide to live up to this identity.

Notice that the disciples were hiding together. This is our indication that they did not merely live with physical fears. If they merely had physical fears for safety, then they would have hidden separately from each other. Instead, they hid together, as a group (minus Thomas). The fact that they hid as a group betrays the concept that individual identity was a component. They had a group identity to protect. They had a group identity that glued them together in one place. They did not go their separate ways, back to their own homes and communities, which arguably would have been a lot less noticeable and therefore a lot safer. Instead, they hid as a group. If they went their separate ways, then each would have to face the scorn of his own community. Each man would have to face an identity crisis on his own.

Can you imagine following a teacher, in this case Jesus, for three and a half years, only to have it all explode in your face? Can you imagine leaving your family, your business, and your future behind, giving it all to Jesus, and then watching him not deliver on all his promises? It all came crashing down in one short day. The Rabbi you followed claimed to be the

Messiah, the one who would deliver the Jewish nation from the Roman Empire. Instead of conquering the Romans, your "fearless leader" was conquered by the Romans, by being hung naked on a cross—the most humiliating death. Jesus claimed to be God's Son, but to be hung on a tree meant that you were actually cursed by God. And God would never curse his own Son, right? Do you know how humiliating it would be to show your face after such a scandal?

No wonder the disciples stuck together. If they returned to their own homes, they would be called failures, losers, idiots, and much worse. Grown men fear such labels. They had to stick together. To go out into the nasty world, even if the Jewish authorities were not hunting them down, would have been social suicide. The disciples were the laughingstock of the region. "Can you believe they gave everything to be with that guy who was convicted and executed? What a waste!" You can hear the townspeople gossip and sneer.

Have you had your reputation slandered? Have others said such devastating things about you? Have you made some poor choices, such that you are afraid of what others will think of you? Are you afraid of being the person they think you are? Are you afraid of being the sort of person you despise? The disciples had almost nothing going for them. They were not only locked in physically, but also socially. Both their necks and their reputations were on the line. No wonder they were crippled with fear. No wonder they hid themselves like criminals after a crime. They were guilty of believing in the latest traveling preacher—one who was seen as a threat to the government. How humiliating and terrifying, all at once.

The Location of Fear

So where is fear? Is fear something that comes from the outside or from the inside? Is fear something that is inflicted upon us or something that is generated within us? I know my answer may be surprising, but I think that fear is generated within us. "But what about those times when we are being chased by a man with a chainsaw?" you retort. "That seems to be external and not just a product of my imagination!" So how can I say that fear is within?

Imagine two teenage girls walking the streets of the Bronx late at night. Suddenly, they notice that a gang of older, young men is following them. The girls walk faster. The gang walks faster. The girls do not know what to do. The gang is closing in on them. They are scared and rightly so. Just as the gang is within a block away, the girls see a 24-hour restaurant and manage to slip inside, unharmed. The gang does not follow them in. The girls are safe. They sigh a breath of relief as the fear leaves.

Now let us replay the situation, using the same gang of young men, the same dark street in the Bronx, and the same late night hour. Only this time, replace the two teenage girls with two adult male police officers who are on patrol. Now who is afraid of whom? Surely the police officers are not crippled by fear like the two girls were? Surely the police officers do not panic and seek shelter in local 24-hour restaurant? In fact, the opposite may be true: the gang of boys might be afraid of the police officers!

So where is fear? Consider a woman named Melba, who lived in a nursing home. Melba had Alzheimer's disease. I served as her Activity Therapist when I was just out of college. Melba was a very sweet old woman. But she was always scared. She would walk up to me multiple times a day, place her hand gently on my arm and whisper, "Honey, I'm so nervous." Her voice trembled. Her gentle blue eyes were full of fear. I would constantly reassure her, "Melba, it's okay, I am right here with you; you need not be afraid." You see nobody else lived in fear like Melba. In fact, some people were happy and some were sad. Only Melba was paralyzed by fear.

87

So where does fear come from? Fear comes from within each individual, as we respond to mental and material stimuli. Why is this important? Because you are not obligated to be paralyzed by fear. If fear is external, then you have no choice. When you are in a scary situation, you must be afraid. But if fear comes from within you, in response to life, then you have some control. Do not hear me wrongly; it is good and healthy to be afraid when the situation calls for it. To preserve your life you must run from the gang of men. But it is not good and healthy to live as if fear is always present. To be "always nervous, honey" is crippling. It is no way to live.

Fear comes from within. You do not have to bow to it always. There can be normalcy. Let us now see how Jesus enters our fears and stands up to them.

Love Drives Out Fear

In another of Saint John's writings, he observes, "Perfect love drives *out* fear" (1 John 4:18, italics mine). Notice that fear is driven out. That means it comes from within, as we observed. Love, according to John, enters into a person with weapons of grace and bullies fear out from under our skin. Love drives out the crippling fear that is within us. One thing is replaced with another.

This fact is key to dealing with fear in your life. Keep in mind that Jesus had other options. The man just overthrew the fiercest enemy that civilizations have ever known: death. Jesus could have continued his rampage and struck the Jewish authorities next, followed by the Romans. Jesus could have gone after the "perceived" cause of fear. But Jesus knows better. Jesus knows that fears are not generated from external sources, like the threatening authorities. He knows that fears come from within. That is why Jesus goes to the source of the fear: the disciples themselves. Jesus breaks into the very nucleus of fear, bearing both scar and Spirit. That is where Jesus makes his stand. He does not stand up against that which the disciples think to be their enemy, namely the authorities. Jesus stands up where the true enemy lurks: within the dark hearts of men who do not trust God to deliver them. In order to release the disciples from crippling fear, he breaks into the walls of fear itself.

Do not expect God to deal with your fears any differently. God does not always work like we want him to. We want him to destroy the external things that are threatening us. Instead, God may choose to work another way. He may choose to get inside of you and replace your fears, which are relative, with peace and the Holy Spirit. He starts the revolution within, not without. His love for you is demonstrated when he drives out your fear, not when he destroys your enemies in an afternoon.

Changing the Fuel

Though the doors were locked for fear of the authorities, Jesus showed up anyway. He did not deal with the authorities; instead he dealt with the disciples. This is a metaphor on how Jesus will help you deal with your fear. Though we want Jesus to drive away the external cause of our fear, he knows better. He knows that the threat on the outside is not the real source of your fear. The fear that is crippling you is coming from within you.

The external threat you are responding to may have been the spark that started the engine, but it is not the fuel that keeps the engine running. External threats such as job loss, loneliness, reputation, and physical security are all sparks. They are not the fuel of your fear. Your fear is fueled by a host of things going on inside of you. The main one, as I see it, is a lack of knowledge of how much you are loved and cherished by God. Perfect love drives *out* fear. You were built to run on perfect love from God, not these foreign fuels from our fallen nature.

So what does Jesus put inside of you? Jesus fills your tank

with courage. This courage has been soaked in the warm love of God. Jesus does not do away with the fears you are hiding from; Jesus gives you the courage to face them.

Peace

There is a song that I often listen to when I am facing enemies at the door. It is a song written by the late Rich Mullins titled *Hold Me, Jesus.* This song does for me what Jesus did for the disciples when he stood up in their fear. Notice the first thing that Jesus says to his scared disciples. "Peace be with you" (John 20:19). Now the song:

> *Hold me, Jesus.*
> *I'm shaking like a leaf.*
> *You have been my King of glory,*
> *Won't you be my Prince of Peace.*

Sometimes we feel like that leaf. We are so tender and vulnerable. We are so weak in the presence of the winds swarming around us. We tremble and shake with fear. We do not want to let go, but the winds might be too much for us. The leaf is just one breath away from being separated from the branch. Sometimes we feel like that, too.

In the midst of all our trembling, we just need someone to hold us and give us peace. When we are paralyzed by fear, we need peace most of all. Mullins knew it; Jesus knew it. Mullins asked Jesus to hold him as he trembled. You can picture a father holding his small child during the middle of the night when that child wakes from a bad dream, trembling in fear. Jesus held the disciples, as his bestowal of peace wrapped itself around them. Notice that Jesus gives them peace not once, but twice. In verse 19, he says, "Peace be with you." In verse 21, he says again, "Peace be with you." It is as if Jesus' peace were holding the disciples, surrounding them as a divine hug. Though they shook like trembling leaves, Jesus held on tightly to them. The first part of his strategy is to give them his peace, as arms around a child.

Scars

The second part of his strategy is to show them his scars. "When he had said this, he showed them his hands and his side" (John 20:20). Jesus was crucified. The Romans drove nails into his hands (his wrists) and feet (a single nail for both overlapping feet). As Saint John recorded in John 19:34, Jesus also had a spear plunged into his side, to ensure his death. The disciples knew the marks of their Master; Jesus felt the need to show them that it was he.

But this went deeper than what dog tags do after battle; it was more than mere identification. This was part of Jesus' strategy of filling the disciples with courage. In the midst of their fears of death and humiliation, Jesus shows them scars of his own death and humiliation. "Are you scared?" we can hear Jesus asking them, "Don't you think that I was scared, too?" Jesus left the security and glory of heaven in order to roam the dark streets of this world. Jesus always knew where his road ended. He knew that at the end of his road he would have to face a Roman cross.

Imagine living your life knowing the future would bring a Roman cross. You would not die comfortably in your bed at home surrounded by your loved ones. You would not die quickly in an unfortunate accident. You would not die in a hospital, as sterile professionals did everything they could to rescue you. You would die on a wicked beam designed to mock and torture. You would die surrounded by enemies who could care less about your comfort, well being, and existential struggles. You would die on a dirty hill, held in the air by rusty nails, which were driven into wood that gave you splinters every time you tried to breathe. Soon your lungs would fill up with juice, your heart would explode, and your side would receive a dagger. Jesus lived every day of his life with this picture in his mind. Yet he lived anyway.

"Don't you realize that I was scared, too?" Jesus said as he showed his scares to his disciples. "I could have been crippled by fear, too. But then I wouldn't have been able to carry out my life's purpose." And Jesus' life purpose was to love the world by giving himself on the cross for those who would believe in him (see John 3:16).

By showing his disciples his scars, he was telling them that they could have courage, too. They need not hide away in fear. They could face their enemies, just like Jesus did. So what if they were mocked? So what if they were killed? Jesus' scars sought to make them brave. Jesus' scars can make you brave, too. Are you facing more than Jesus faced? Will you be scarred more than he? As Jesus shows you his scars, may he show you the courage you need to face your enemies.

And may you also have the courage to show your own scars to those around you. You may think that nothing good can come from your wounds. You may think it best to keep your past covered up. But your scars could be a great source of courage to someone else. When you talk about your struggles in just the right place at just the right time, your story could bring hope into another person's life. Even now, God might be causing somebody to come to mind that you could share with. Even now, God could be using you to give someone else courage when they need it the most. That is what Jesus' scars can do for you; and that is what your scars can do for another.

The Great Commission

Indeed, that is the sort of ministry that Jesus is calling you to. "As the Father has sent me, even so I am sending you" (John 20:21). The Father sent the Son to heal the world with his scars. The Father sent the Son to absorb the pain of the world with his body and soul. The point of absorption was the cross, when the Son soaked up every sin that would keep us from spending eternity with a Holy God. Like a sponge, he drew out our sin from the past, the present, and the future. All of his people's sin was absorbed by the only One unsaturated enough to handle it. Once absorbed, Jesus took our sin to the grave and buried it. He beat it down until it was finally dead, and then stood up himself to announce our release.

Our forgiveness was not cheap. It cost God a Son and it cost the Son his life. Wrath against our sin is what pinned him to the cross and pushed him to the grave. If you are forgiven, then God holds nothing against you anymore. If you are forgiven, then the Father holds all of your sin against the Son. His Son Jesus claims full responsibility for your sin so that you can walk free. You are completely blameless in the Father's eyes (see 1 Thessalonians 5:23).

That is how the Father sent the Son. He sent the Son to absorb sin and announce forgiveness. That is how the Son sends his followers. Jesus stood up in the disciples' locked place, showed his scars, and then told them that they must go out and offer forgiveness to the world. That was their mission. Soon the followers of Jesus would have their own scars to show, as they absorbed hatred from persecutors. Their job was to tell the world that the blood of Jesus could clean our conscience. "If you forgive the sins of any, they are forgiven them; if you withhold the forgiveness from any, it is withheld" (John 20:23).

In the past, only God could forgive sins. Then Jesus showed up claiming to have the same authority (see Mark 2:10). Now he gives this authority to forgive sins to the disciples, who represent the church. These few timid disciples have the authority that once was reserved only for God himself. Their job was to tell the world that the solution it needs is found in Jesus the Messiah. Jesus takes away the sin of the world by nailing it to the cross. As the disciples learned to proclaim the death and resurrection of Jesus, little resurrections were happening everywhere. Soon hundreds, thousands, and millions of people would stand up in victory, just like Jesus.

The scared disciples had a mission to carry out. They could not remain crippled by fear. In order to escape their own pain, Jesus was calling them to absorb the pain of the world with the sponge of the gospel. The gospel is the "good news" that Jesus put our sins to death and rose to give us new life.

Holy Spirit

To accomplish this mission, Jesus gives the Holy Spirit. The Holy Spirit is a Person. The God of the Bible represents himself as a Father, a Son, and a Holy Spirit. God is One Being but three Persons. There are no adequate analogies to express this divine community. There is only one God. But this God has a love-relationship built into his being. It is the love relationship between the Father, Son, and Holy Spirit. That is how God can be personal. When Christians say that God wants to have a personal relationship with you, it is because he can! The Father sent the Son to minister personally. The Father and Son send the Holy Spirit to minister personally.

The Holy Spirit is also called the Comforter. It is fascinating to look at both the Greek and Latin roots of the word "comfort." In Greek, comfort is made up of two words that mean, "come alongside" and "call out." To comfort is to come alongside and call out. In Latin, comfort is made up of two words that mean, "with" and "strength." Putting the two definitions together gives us a beautiful analogy of what it means to comfort: to come alongside and call out words with strength. The Holy Spirit is the divine person who comes alongside of you, wherever you are at, and calls out words of strength. "You can do it!" "You are going to be okay!" "You are going to make it!" "You are loved!" "You are appreciated!" "You are needed!"

Just when we want to give up, the Holy Spirit will whisper words of strength to us. He will get down on the ground alongside of us, when we are stuck in the mud and trapped in our fears. He will call out to us when we are about to collapse, or quit, or worse.

The 2006 film *Facing the Giants* has a stirring scene, which illustrates this idea. At the end of a hard practice, the coach has a kid named Brock Kelley do the "death crawl." The death crawl consisted of walking on your hands and feet down the field with someone on your back like a horse with its rider draped across its back. Before Brock did the death crawl, his coach put a blindfold on him so he could not see how far he was going. Brock put a 160-pound teammate on his back and began the death crawl down the field. Brock thought he could only make it 30 yards—if that. But wearing the blindfold, he actually had no idea of how far he went. As Brock crawled, the coach cheered him on. The coach went with him every step of the way. The coach was not tame, either. He threw himself on the ground right next to Brock. Coach slammed his hand against the grass over and over again, calling out words like, "Don't quit, Brock! Don't quit!" As the scene progressed, so did the drama. Brock wanted to quit, but coach would not let him. "I can't!" Brock would say. Coach would yell back, "You can! You can!" He put his face in Brock's face. "Ten more yards, Brock!" "Don't quit on me until you have nothing left!" "Don't quit on me, Brock. Don't Quit!" "Don't quit until you have nothing left!" Coach repeatedly shouted such words of strength to Brock. By the time Brock finally collapsed, he was in the in-zone. He had made it not just 30 yards, but 100. It was all because his coach walked with him and cheered him on.

That is what the Holy Spirit is like. The Holy Spirit goes with you every step of the way and calls out words of strength in your ear. When you are blind to what is going on, when it feels like you are doing the death crawl, the Holy Spirit will not let you crawl by yourself. He will give you an earful of strength. His words will be your strength. His promises to be with you will get you through. He will not let you give up. He is pounding the grass alongside of you, shouting, "Don't quit! Don't quit!"

Hear the shouts of the Holy Spirit more than the shouts of the enemy at your door. The Spirit will walk out of your locked place with you. The Comforter will surround you with peace and fill you with courage. He will remind you that you are loved and forgiven, and that you have a job to do for Jesus. It is not just your mission; it is the Spirit's mission, too. It is a commission. God goes with you into the scary world, where everything seems to be on the line.

Joy

When Jesus stands up in your locked place, he turns your fear into joy. "Then the disciples were *glad* when they saw the Lord" (John 20:20, italics mine). Literally, it says, "the disciples rejoiced." Crouching in fear, they suddenly leapt with joy.

Joy is the replacement of fear. When fear leaves, joy follows closely behind. Imagine the joy that one experiences when he finds out that the scratching at the window is not an intruder, but a tree branch. Imagine the joy that one experiences when she finds out that she was not rejected, but accepted into the college of her dreams. Imagine the joy that one experiences when he finds out that his team held the line, recovered the fumble, and scored the winning touchdown.

One can go from being crippled by fear to hilarious joy in an instant. When it finally dawned on the disciples that their friend Jesus stood alive before them, joy erupted. I am sure that some of them even applauded. Joy runs silently at the heels of fear, ready to replace it.

Just as fear comes from within, so does joy. We learned earlier that fear comes from an internal source rather than an external source. In the same way, joy comes from within us, rather than from our circumstances. This is good news. *This means that we can have joy no matter what is going on around us.* Keep in mind that the disciples still had enemies outside of their home; Jesus did not deal with their enemies at this point. He just stood up. But his standing in their midst was enough to catapult them out of fear and into joy. Just as fear came from within them, so did joy.

If you are paralyzed by fear right now, please do not lose heart. Joy may be closer than you think. Even when you cry, you could be on the verge of laughter. The disciples were afraid of death and they were afraid of shame. That is why they locked themselves together in one place. But Jesus stood up in the middle of their crippled condition. The miracle of the stand introduced a new category all together. This new category was that of the impossible. Against all odds, the impossible happened. Though his body was butchered by the authorities, Jesus stood in complete defiance of human possibilities. His stand was impossible. But Jesus did the impossible anyway.

Recall that fear is our internal response to something in the future that threatens us. We fear something that might happen to us in the future. *When Jesus stood up among them, he brought the future into the present.* Jesus' stand proclaimed to the disciples, "This is what your future holds!" Their future would not end in death or shame, but life and glory. After all that was done to Jesus' body and reputation, his future was that of victory. Life was in Jesus' future. No matter what would happen to the disciples, life would be in their future, too. Jesus showed them how it would end. It all ends in resurrection. Death is replaced with life. That is how Jesus' stand can replace fear with joy. That's what Saint Paul meant when he wrote, "Death is swallowed up in victory" (1 Corinthians 15:54).

The future of darkness is light. That fact will give you courage to step outside and face your enemies, for they will not win.

This is the sixth reason why you must not give up: you are released from fear.

Reason #7:

You Are Released from Doubt

Now Thomas, one of the Twelve, called the Twin, was not with them when Jesus came. So the other disciples told him, "We have seen the Lord." But he said to them, "Unless I see in his hands the mark of the nails, and place my finger into the mark of the nails, and place my hand into his side, I will never believe." Eight days later, his disciples were inside again, and Thomas was with them. Although the doors were locked, Jesus came and stood among them and said, "Peace be with you." Then he said to Thomas, "Put your finger here, and see my hands; and put out your hand, and place it in my side. Do not disbelieve, but believe." Thomas answered him, "My Lord and my God!" Jesus said to him, "Have you believed because you have seen me? Blessed are those who have not seen and yet have believed."
~ John 20:24-29

Hiding behind Questions

After seeing how Jesus' resurrection has the ability to release us from sorrow and from fear, we now turn to doubt. We will discover that the resurrection can also release us from

99

doubt. We saw that Mary was trapped by sorrow and the disciples were paralyzed by fear. In this chapter we will discover how Thomas was infected by doubt. We move from the garden to the home to the mind, as we move from Mary to the disciples to Thomas.

Just as Jesus was able to stand up in the garden and in the house, he is also able to stand up in our doubts. Jesus can stand up to your disbelief. Jesus is not afraid of your skepticism; he does not hide from your questions. The opposite is true: *we tend to hide behind our questions.* But Jesus, the all-knowing God, will not let us hide.

Many do not struggle with sorrow or fear; many wrestle with doubt. You are constantly questioning your beliefs. Are my beliefs true or do I believe the wrong thing? Will there be consequences for what I believe? How can I know that God exists? Can I just have a little more proof? Then we turn our questions into a conditional statement. *If* I have more evidence, *then* I will believe. That is how we hide behind our questions. Instead of embracing belief, we procrastinate with questioning. Unless I have my questions answered and my doubts dispelled, I will not believe. We cannot see things any other way. It is as simple and straightforward as that. Our thinking is "infected" by this sort of reasoning. We cannot think about God any other way. It makes no sense to embrace Jesus when I have so many unanswered questions.

Some have legitimate doubts. But others use their doubts as an excuse, a place of hiding. I was talking to my coworker Rodney one day about faith. I asked him if he went to church. He said, "There are so many people who believe in God, but live lousy lives. I've just been hurt by way too many people who claimed to be Christians."

"That's not what I asked," I continued. "I asked if you went to church. I didn't ask about your evaluation of Christians." Rodney gave a half-smile. Quickly, I added, "Have you ever wrecked your car? Or has your car ever broken down?"

"Why, sure!" Rodney exclaimed. "I've gotten in so many car wrecks, especially when I was a teenager!"

"Then I can assume that you walked to work today?" I responded.

"No, I drove—why would I walk?" he asked.

"If you had so many bad experiences with cars, then why didn't you give up on them?" I said. "The truth is that cars have a high priority in your life. And you will do almost whatever it takes to keep driving. One little wreck or one blown head gasket will not stop you from driving, because driving is important to you. Rodney, if you're honest with yourself, the reason why you gave up on the church is not because parts of it were wrecked, but because it's just not that important to you." He smiled all the way. He knew what I was getting at. Just to be clear, I added, "If God were important to you, then you would do whatever it takes to help your relationship with him. You wouldn't quit simply because you had a bad experience or because someone hurt you."

We are like Rodney so much of the time. We hide behind our excuses and our experiences. We justify our lack of faith because of something that has happened to us.

Another friend of mine, named Pete, had a similar struggle. I asked him if he believed in God. Pete said that he could not believe in God because of all the pain that he has been through in his life. That is understandable, but it is not excusable. Just because I go through trials does not mean that God does not exist. The same could be true of the opposite: just because I go through prosperity does not mean that God does exist. God's existence is not contingent on our experiences. Actually, our experiences are contingent on God's existence! More important, it is dangerous to base your belief in God on hurt that has been done to you.

In no way am I minimizing your pain. Remember what

101

we learned in chapter three: God weeps over your pain. Your pain is not good at all - in fact it is horrible. But it is tragic when our pain is allowed to damage not only our spirit, but also our mind. We give pain too many rights when we allow it the freedom of dictating what we do or do not believe. Pain has done enough damage. We do not need to let it hurt our beliefs, too. Instead of saying, "Because there are so many rotten Christians, I will not be a part of a church," we could say, "Even though there are so many rotten Christians, I will be different." Instead of saying, "Because so many bad things happen, I will not believe in God," we could say, "Because so many bad things happen, I must rely on God to make the world right."

For most of us, the issue is not whether the God of the Bible could logically exist or not. For most of us, the issue is our pain. We withhold belief not because it seems illogical, but because we are hurting. I would wager that most atheists have had something terrible happen to them; and that terrible event is the root cause of their atheism. Of course, an atheist might argue similarly, "The only reason he can believe in God is because nothing bad has happened to him." That is fair. But it still supports my conclusion that we tend to base our beliefs on the pain we experience or do not experience. My argument is that experience infects our beliefs, positively or negatively.

The question changes from "What can I do about my doubts?" to "Why do I doubt?" Do I doubt because of something that has happened (or not happened) to me? Do I lack faith because of some pain that I had to struggle through? Can I trace my disbelief back to hurtful words or actions spoken or done against me? Why do I doubt? Why is my thinking infected with disbelief? What first caused the infection?

I want to believe, but it is just too hard. It is as if my mind will not allow me to do so. I just cannot get beyond what happened to me. I just cannot see past the atrocity that happened to those people. I just cannot move forward knowing that those kinds of so-called "believers" are out there, ruining lives.

Hurt

Hurt. That is where Thomas was. Jokingly, he is known as "Doubting Thomas." We assume that his doubts were merely cognitive—Thomas was just a logical guy who needed logical answers. But Thomas does not display logic in John 20:24-29; he displays hurt. Thomas has been hurt by Jesus; that is the reason for his disbelief. Perhaps it is better to call him "Hurting Thomas." Let me show you why I think this to be the case.

When Thomas declares Jesus to be "my Lord and my God" (John 20:28), he is referring to Jesus' personal faithfulness. Jesus is not just anyone's Lord and God; he is Thomas' personal Lord and God. This means that before his realization and declaration, Thomas struggled with Jesus' personal faithfulness. When Thomas calls Jesus Lord and God, he was referring to Jesus' as "The God Who Is There," as that is a fair rendering of what "Lord" and "God" mean together. Jesus is not just the powerful God, but he is also the present Lord. He is faithful. He is by your side through thick and thin. He is there for you to rely on. He is trustworthy and will get you through. When Jesus stood up alive, Thomas realized that Jesus was indeed still there for him. Jesus was still present, even though death snatched him away for a bit. Jesus returned. Now Thomas could see that Jesus was One who could be trusted and relied upon. Jesus was both a powerful God and a present Lord.

All this means, nonetheless, that before Jesus stood up (before his resurrection), Thomas had stopped believing in Jesus as present and powerful. Thomas had stopped believing that Jesus was trustworthy and reliable. After all, Jesus walked out on them. Jesus claimed to be somebody, but it turns out that he was just like everybody else—or so Thomas thought.

Thomas' doubt, therefore, was not merely cognitive, but emotive. Thomas was hurt by Jesus. Jesus, as Thomas thought, was just another pretender. Jesus was nobody special. Though everyone thought that Jesus was the messiah, a messiah does not abandon his kingdom like Jesus did. A true messiah fights and endures through thick and thin. A true messiah achieves the victory, overcomes all opposition, and remains to rule his kingdom. But Jesus was defeated on the cross, was overcome by the Romans, and left for the grave. Jesus walked out on his disciples and all those who had placed so much hope in him. They thought that he would be the one, but he turned out to be a fraud.

I am sure that you can relate to Thomas' hurt. Did you have someone walk out on you? Do you feel like you have been abandoned? Did you have large expectations for someone, only to be let down by that same person? Did you look up to somebody for years, only to be hurt by him in a single day? Did she turn out to be a fraud? Did he make promises that he did not keep? Have you been hurt like Thomas?

This is why Thomas doubted. Jesus hurt him. Jesus did not overthrow the Romans, as was expected. Even more, Jesus was humiliated by the Romans. Jesus was the laughing stock. Jesus was slaughtered like a piece of meat and then hung on a tree as a curse (cf. Deuteronomy 21:22-23). Jesus proved to be anything but the messiah. Jesus was neither a powerful God nor a present Lord. For Jesus was defeated and departed. There is no such thing, Thomas reasoned, as a Lord who leaves. A crucified God is an oxymoron. If he really were God, then he could not and would not be crucified by pagans. Thomas' doubt flowed from his hurt.

Revenge

There is another reason why I think that Thomas' doubt was driven by emotional hurt. You see this in Thomas' cruel request of Jesus. This cruel request is more than passive aggression. Thomas is hurt and he strikes back at the one who abandoned them. How does Thomas strike back? First, notice that Thomas was not present with the rest of the disciples at

Jesus' earlier visit. "Now Thomas, one of the Twelve…was not with them when Jesus came [at first]" (John 20:24). Thomas withdrew. That was passive aggression toward Jesus.

Second, his passive aggression turns active when he makes a morbid request. His morbid request turns Jesus into an animal at best and an object at worst. Thomas asks to violate the body of Jesus by thrusting his hand into his wounds. That is disturbing. That is Thomas' revenge. "You claimed to be somebody special, Jesus. But then you left us high and dry. I will not honor you as a messiah, but as an ordinary piece of flesh." Thomas sought to make Jesus un-special, common, and profane. You worship God, you do not pick at him like a vulture does carrion.

If Thomas merely had intellectual issues, just seeing Jesus would have been enough to believe. Thomas could have said, "Unless I see Jesus for myself, then I will not believe." But Thomas did not say that. Notice the progression of his revenge in verse 25. First, he says, "Unless I see in his hands the mark of the nails." He starts by requesting to see Jesus' scars. Thomas does not stop there - he goes further. Second, he says, "And place my finger into the mark of the nails." Now he wants to poke at Jesus' wounds, like a scientist pokes a specimen on the lab table. Just in case you have missed it, imagine asking an amputee if you could rub the spot where the arm used to be. Such a request would not be well received. Third, if his last request were not enough, Thomas drives the emotional knife in further by stating, "And 'place' my hand into his side." Thomas literally asks to "throw" his hand into the right side of Jesus where the Roman executioners "threw" the sword. Like the Romans wounded Jesus, so did Thomas want to wound Jesus. As I alluded to in chapter five, hurt people hurt people.

This was Thomas' revenge. I do not want to be too hard on Thomas, however. I am sure that I would not have reacted much kinder. It hurts when someone leaves. It hurts

105

when parents break up and loved ones depart because of death. Dealing with death and separation is hard enough. There is no need to start making jokes about a body coming back to life. That does not help me in my grief. Are you trying to get my hopes up again? Do you want to see my hopes come crashing down a second time when he leaves again? When I realize that it is not true?

Disbelief is More Disturbing

The atmosphere that Saint John paints is disturbing. This whole brief scene is quite unsettling. There are four reasons given by the text.

First, the reader asks herself, "Why was Thomas missing to begin with?" As I mentioned above, that is unsettling. Keep in mind that the only other disciple who was missing was the one who betrayed Jesus, Judas Iscariot. Judas has a horrible reputation at this point. He is the one who colluded with the Jewish authorities to kill Jesus; he is the one who betrayed the Son of God for thirty pieces of silver; and he is the one who was overwhelmed with guilt and committed suicide. It is understandable why Judas is missing from the Twelve. But Thomas? By noting that Thomas is missing, John lumps him together with Judas. I am not saying that Thomas did the crimes that Judas did, but by noting that Thomas was away from the rest, the reader is to see a link between Thomas and Judas. Both were away from the rest. Judas had his reasons and Thomas had his. Though it is not stated why Thomas was missing, the evidence suggests that his relationship with Jesus was damaged, as was Judas.' It is disturbing to be associated with Judas Iscariot.

Second, the reader asks herself, "Why was Thomas so morbid?" As discussed above, Thomas was flat out vulgar with Jesus.[1] Thomas' requests do quite a bit to add to the disturbing

---

[1] *Larry Darnell George, Reading the Tapestry (New York: Peter Lang, 2000), 99.*

atmosphere painted in these verses.

Third, the reader asks herself, "Why could not the disciples convince their close friend of Jesus' resurrection?" It is unsettling that such a close group of friends could not convince Thomas of what they saw. On the one hand, why was Thomas so distrusting? On the other hand, why were the disciples unable to reach out to their friend and convince him of what they saw?

Fourth, the reader asks herself, "Why were the disciples still behind closed doors?" After we left the last scene, it was assumed that the disciple's fear was dealt with. Jesus gave to them the Holy Spirit. Jesus gave them astounding authority and courage. And they are still scared? It has been a week and they are still behind closed doors? What is going on? Something is not quite right with this picture. This last piece of evidence adds even further to the unsettling feeling of this passage.

None of these four reasons is conclusive. You could argue any one of these reasons another way. None are totally wrong. The scene is not outright hopeless. By adding all four together, however, one must admit that something is not quite right. You may not be able to put your finger on it (sorry, Thomas!) but you have an unsettled sense. Where was Thomas? Why does a disciple of Jesus say such vulgar things? Why couldn't his friends help him to believe? Why were they all still in their home? Didn't Jesus give them a job to do?

This leads to major point about disbelief. Disbelief is disturbing. It is unsettling. John paints an unsettling atmosphere to let us know that it is not "normal" to disbelieve God.

I have to be careful here. After all, this book is supposed to give you hope, not tear you down because of your beliefs. Here I am telling you that you are precious and loved on the one hand, but "not normal" and "disturbing" on the other!

Am I speaking out of both sides of my mouth?

You may be struggling right now with doubt. By now, you have begun to understand that a lot of our doubt comes from past experiences of hurt. Hurting people sometimes turns into doubting people. In no way do I want to bury you even more in hopelessness by saying that you are both hurt and wrong.

What I want to do is recognize what John is telling us in these verses. I want these verses to be a wake-up call for both you and I. For John challenges our assumptions. We assume that since we have been hurt, God has to prove himself to us to get us to trust him again. We assume that God is disturbing, but John says the opposite. John says that we are disturbing. John says that our requests to make God prove himself to us are unsettling. Why does God have to justify himself? A king does not have to explain all of his ways to peasants in the field. His ways are beyond their understanding.

God has given us the world. Is that not enough? Do we still question his goodness? God gave us the ability to be. God gave us soil to walk upon, air to breathe, and food to eat. God clothes us, cares for us, and holds our bodies together. God shaped our passions, showed us pleasures, and shared his plans for us. He gave us a moral code to live by. He installed a conscience within each one of us. He tells us of his love for us in his Holy Scriptures. He searches for us when we are lost, disciplines us when we need to learn, and sends angels to us when we need to be led. Something good is happening in this world; your greatest enemy has been defeated; you are loved; someone stands for you; you are released from sorrow; and you are released from fear. Has not God done enough?

It is unsettling to live as if God needs to do more. It is unsettling to doubt our Creator. It is disturbing to distrust the One who faithfully gives us each breath, so that we do not have to worry about both reading and breathing right now. John

108

makes the same point earlier in his book when he describes the "reception" that God received when he came to earth as Jesus. "He was in the world, and the world was made through him, yet the world did not know him. He came to his own, and his own people did not receive him" (John 1:10-11).

Jesus stands up to such doubts. Yes, Jesus does love us and tenderly care for us. But there comes a time when we need to hear that our doubts are disturbing. There comes a time when someone needs to stand up and say that it is not right to be vulgar with God. There comes a time when we need to start disbelieving our disbeliefs.

My prayer is that hearing that will relieve you. It is exhausting to fight against God. It is disturbing to live each day with the infection of doubt. I hope that these words will be bold enough to serve as antibodies to your doubt. Doubt may be fine to a point. But if left untreated for too long, a dangerous infection might settle in.

Compassion

Though God does not need to prove himself to us, especially when we are vulgar, he does anyway. How gentle and loving God is with us! Though my words were firm, his are tender. The word "compassion" literally means, "to suffer with" another. Jesus had compassion on Thomas. Thomas was suffering from hurt and doubt. Jesus got down on Thomas' level and suffered with him. Jesus suffered the humiliation of subjecting his body to the morbid desires of a faithless creature, Thomas. Jesus met Thomas where he was, in other words.

Keep in mind that Jesus had every right to discipline Thomas at this point. Jesus could have put Thomas in his place with words like, "You arrogant mortal! How dare you make morbid demands of me, rather than worshiping me as I deserve!" After all, Jesus was perfect and he just defeated death. Nobody had a resume like his. A perfect Being is approached

109

humbly, reverently, with fear and with trembling. Thomas was much too flippant, sarcastic, and profane. Thomas approached Jesus with no faith. Thomas began as a nonbeliever. Jesus did not have to put up with his attitude, requests, or behavior.

Jesus made a special trip for Thomas. Thomas was hurting. He was suffering. Jesus came "eight days later" to give compassion to Thomas (John 21:26). Jesus came to "suffer with" this hurting disciple. Jesus met Thomas right where Thomas was —literally and emotionally. Jesus shows great accommodation. If Thomas needed a vulgar display in order to believe, then that is what Jesus would give him.

Then [Jesus] said to Thomas, "Put your finger here, and see my hands; and put out your hand, and place it in my side." ~ John 20:27

Jesus accommodated to a hurting human by subjecting himself to Thomas' special requests. Jesus was not too holy to do that. In fact, his holiness drove him to do it, for holiness seeks to be spread. Holiness wants to make believers out of us all. "Do not disbelieve, but believe."

Notice that Jesus is omniscient. He showed up, knowing what Thomas' request was. Notice also that the whole point of Jesus' accommodation was to stimulate faith. God gets down on our level in order to stimulate fresh faith. Jesus does not accommodate just so we will be impressed with his humility. Jesus does not accommodate just to give us a kind of freak show. Jesus does not accommodate just to ease our suffering, a shoulder rub when life is bumpy. He accommodates to us so that we will become believers. He comes to us so that we will come to him, so that we can come to him.

Or, to use the metaphor of the resurrection again, Jesus stands up next to us, in our hurting place, so that we can stand up, too. He gives us what we need to stand in our faith. Jesus

110

stands before us, showing us his wounds and offering us his side, if that is what it takes to cause his newborn lambs to rise-up on trembling legs.

This is the great secret of believing in Jesus. This is the moment that sets this whole thing apart. Nobody is ready for it; nobody expects it; and nobody knows why. God does not wait for you to dry your tears, deal with your hurt, and do something wonderful. You do not have to show your faith before he comes after you. God does not wait for you to come to him. God comes to you first. God is not up in heaven waiting for you to get your act together. He barges into your room, gets down on his knees, throws open his shirt, and commands you to feel the scars that made you his.

This means that you cannot earn a spot next to Jesus. Your astounding faith or good deeds do not make you right with God. Jesus comes and finds his spot next to you. Jesus' astounding faith and good deeds make you right with God. You need only to let him show you his love for you. He does not hide his love from you. God does not leave you wondering where he stands with you. God does not leave you alone in your doubts. God comes inside of your doubts and meets you where you are.

Recall how Jesus met Mary right where she was. To Mary, Jesus said, "Do not hold onto me" (John 20:17). But to Thomas, Jesus basically says, "Hold on to me!" Why does Jesus use two different approaches? Because Mary and Thomas are two different people. This demonstrates that Jesus meets us where we are, and never the reverse. We do not have to meet Jesus where He is. We do not find him in heaven; he finds us on earth—among the dead and behind deadbolts.

Hope Is Here

We have been waiting our whole lives to hear that hope is available to us. We do not have to strive for it, achieve it,

111

pay for it, or pilgrimage for it. We do not have to be special people or have terrific circumstances. We do not have to have eyes to see and we do not even have to have faith. Hope is a free gift, given to us. We can be locked in the darkest corner of our lives and hope is still there, kneeling in compassion by our side. Our circumstances can be horrible; we can be blind and faithless doubters; we can even be vulgar. Yet, hope stands ready and waiting for us. Hope is always there for us. "Do not disbelieve, but believe" (John 20:26).

This means that the ball is in our court. Jesus has done everything to make hope stand for us. He has knocked away all our excuses, gotten down on our level, and required nothing from us. He stands before us with arms open and scars displayed, as if to show us his great love and welcome us home. We only have two real options at this point. We can either refuse him or worship him. Jesus' breathtaking display of compassionate love leaves us no other options. Either we tell him, "No thanks," and continue to be vulgar, or we fall on our faces like Thomas and exclaim, "My Lord and my God!" (John 20:28).

The resurrection not only makes hope free and available, but also makes God tangible. God does not want to be abstract to you. God is neither a Being too far off to hold nor a concept too hard to grasp. God is as close as your hurt and as touchable as a hand. The resurrection makes hope solid and three-dimensional. Hope is something that is real. Hope is something that lives and breathes. Hope gets down on our level, able to fit right where we need it. Hope is a life that walks and a love that talks. Hope is not fleeting. Hope is here to stay. Death itself could not kill hope. Hope stood up anyway. Hope is not going anywhere, no matter how much you doubt.

Proof

The Resurrection has both subjective impact and objective proof. Saint John includes both components in his account. So far we have been thinking about the subjective impact. The resurrection has an efficacious power that rescues us from our human conditions. The Resurrection also has objective proof. You may be struggling with the facts of the Resurrection. Did the Resurrection really happen? Can we be sure? Do we have sufficient evidence? *(While I will list some evidences here, a fuller list can be found in the appendix of this book.)*

I hope that by now you realize that you are not alone in your struggle. Mary, the disciples, and Thomas all struggled with the Resurrection. None of them figured it out right away. In fact, in each circumstance, Saint John gives evidence of this "process of recognition." In each case, the witnesses (Mary, the disciples, and Thomas) go from sight to sight. Namely, though they see Jesus at first (Mary in John 20:14, the disciples in John 20:19, and Thomas in John 20:26), they do not believe at first. Though they see Jesus in plain sight, they do not believe it is he. Only after Jesus gives a special sign do they believe.

Let us consider these special signs. To Mary, Jesus gave two angels and his own voice. Once she had both signs, she believed. These signs were the pieces of evidence that she needed in order to believe. To the disciples, Jesus had to show them his hands and his side. Once they saw these two pieces of evidence, they believed. To Thomas, Jesus gave his hands and side to touch. Once he had these two pieces of evidence, he believed. Once Mary, the disciples, and Thomas had the signs, they "saw" completely; that is, they believed.

Here is the point. The evidence led to belief, not the other way around. Remember, these witnesses were trapped in an emotional condition that they could not shake on their own. They were not "on the edge of belief," as some have suggested. They were not even looking to believe. They were mourning, hiding, and bitter. Believing in a Resurrected Jesus was the last thing on their minds. They neither had the categories for belief in a Resurrected Messiah nor the emotional capital to start. They were depleted and hopeless. They had no agenda but to figure out how to put life back together again after a horrifying week—if they could even do that.

The human condition was the starting point, not belief. Just because they lived in Ancient Rome does not mean that they naturally believed in tall tales and ghosts. They still needed evidence, just like us. They still struggled to know the next step, as would we. They still saw little logic in it all, just like us. The point once again is that God rescues us from where we are trapped, not the other way around. We do not rescue Jesus from the tomb of rock. The reverse is true. He rescues us from our tombs of sorrow, fear, and doubt. We do not bring him out alive by believing hard enough. He brings us out by standing up in the middle of all our doubts. His stand is a proof so that we can trust him. His Resurrection is a sign for us to believe (John 20:30-31).

The point is that these signs were enough to convince the early followers of Jesus of his resurrection. They did not enter the grave site expecting a resurrection. The signs convinced them. The signs had to be very impressive to cause these first disciples such a radical change of mind. The Resurrection, therefore, is built on evidence, not imagination. From the start, the Resurrection depended on objective evidence. Otherwise, belief would have never happened. Given all of this, the burden of proof is shifted to those who do not believe in the Resurrection to come up with a better explanation for the birth of the church 2,000 years ago. What huge event happened to cause such massive change? If not the Resurrection, then what?[2]

---

[2] *Tim Keller, The Reason for God (New York: Dutton, 2008).*

Your Turn

John believed because he saw the grave clothes. Mary believed because she heard Jesus' voice. The disciples believed because they saw the scars. Thomas believed because he was allowed to touch the scars. Notice how the signs escalate, from clothes to hearing to seeing to touching. But even "touching" is not the climax. John has one more step to add. John wants one more person to believe: you. "Blessed are those who have not seen and yet believed" (John 20:29). You have not had the privilege of seeing Jesus' clothes, hearing his voice, seeing his scars, or touching his wounds. Nonetheless, Jesus wants you to believe, too.

What is your sign? After all, each person got a piece of evidence or sign that catapulted him or her from sight to sight, doubt to belief. What has Jesus left for you and me? John answers that two verses later,

>   *But these are written that you may believe that Jesus is the Christ, the Son of God, and that believing you may have life in his name.* ~ John 20:31

Your sign is the words written by John. Our evidence is the Bible. We may not be eyewitnesses, but we are "ear witnesses."[3] We have not seen Jesus with our own eyes, but we have heard from him through his faithful witnesses, as recorded in Holy Scripture.

It is your turn to believe. You are the climax. Jesus was speaking about you. You are the one who is more "blessed" than Mary, the disciples, or Thomas. This moment was made for you. God wants to give you life in his name. Recall how Thomas' confession was very personal, marked by the two pronouns "my." My Lord and my God. We need to make it personal, too. We need to cry out for Jesus to be our personal Lord and personal God.

[3] *Eckhard Schnabel, Early Christian Mission: Jesus and the Twelve (Downers Grove: IVP, 2004).*

115

It is our turn to be blessed. Did you know that right now you are "more blessed?" You are more blessed than those who actually saw Jesus' physical body. Do you realize how blessed you are? Why are you so blessed? Because you have life in his name. Do not ever forget that you have life. You are not hopeless. There are no more dead ends in Jesus. This is the seventh reason why you must not give up: you are released from doubt.

Reason #8:

Your Future Is Not Failure

After this Jesus revealed himself again to the disciples by the Sea of Tiberias, and he revealed himself in this way. Simon Peter, Thomas (called the Twin), Nathanael of Cana in Galilee, the sons of Zebedee, and two others of his disciples were together. Simon Peter said to them, "I am going fishing." They said to him, "We will go with you." They went out and got into the boat, but that night they caught nothing. Just as day was breaking, Jesus stood on the shore; yet the disciples did not know that it was Jesus. Jesus said to them, "Children, do you have any fish?" They answered him, "No." He said to them, "Cast the net on the right side of the boat, and you will find some." So they cast it, and now they were not able to haul it in, because of the quantity of fish. That disciple whom Jesus loved therefore said to Peter, "It is the Lord!" When Simon Peter heard that it was the Lord, he put on his outer garment, for he was stripped for work, and threw himself into the sea. The other disciples came in the boat, dragging the net full of fish, for they were not far from the land, but about a hundred yards off.

117

When they got out on land, they saw a charcoal fire in place, with fish laid out on it, and bread. Jesus said to them, "Bring some of the fish that you have just caught." So Simon Peter went aboard and hauled the net ashore, full of large fish, 153 of them. And although there were so many, the net was not torn. Jesus said to them, "Come and have breakfast." Now none of the disciples dared ask him, "Who are you?" hey knew it was the Lord. Jesus came and took the bread and gave it to them, and so with the fish. This was now the third time that Jesus was revealed to the disciples after he was raised from the dead.
~ John 21:1-14

Where Hope Is Found

"It would be so much easier to have faith if I didn't have all of these struggles."

"I could have hope were it not for the present circumstances that I am in."

"I would want to go on if the future did not look so bleak."

We think that our faith would be better or stronger if we did not have to struggle. We assume that our lack of hope comes from the presence of enemies and dismal circumstances. Our mind tells us that it is useless to believe until we have reason to do so. In this chapter, we will learn that Jesus not only gives us a reason to have hope in the middle of our failure, but also He provides for us while we are in our need. Jesus' Resurrection plants life in the middle of our failure. He does not avoid it, but rescues it.

Think about Mary, the disciples, and Thomas from John 20. When did hope stand up in their situations? Before? After? When the pain was resolved?

Hope stands when our struggles are ripe and at their climax. Hope does not enter once we figure out a plan; hope enters when we are at our wits end. Hope does not enter when the trial takes a turn for the better; hope stands when we have nowhere else to turn. Here is the key: hope enters when there is a struggle. In other words, hope needs the struggle to be there. That is when hope stands the tallest, when it towers in the face of our enemies.

Hope is not found in our successes, but in our failures. You need to hear that. We think that our failures are a sign that hope is gone. The reality is, our failures are a sign that hope is near. Hope travels with failure, ready to stand tall at just the right moment. Instead of saying, "It would be so much easier to have faith if I didn't have all of these struggles," we must learn to say, "I would not have strong faith if I didn't have all of these struggles." Failure is a breeding ground for hope. We are on the verge of a miraculous catch of fish, and we do not even realize it.

Do Not Miss the Miracle

When we do not realize this, we are in danger of missing the miracle. As we read over John 21:1-14, we assume that there is just one miracle: the large catch of fish. But there is not just one miracle. There is another. Saint John wants to make sure that we do not miss it. It is so important that he wraps the text up with it. He begins this story with it and ends this story with it. In John 21:1, John writes, *"After this Jesus revealed himself again to the disciples by the Sea of Tiberias, and he revealed himself in this way"* Then in John 21:14 at the end of the story, John writes, "This was now the third time that Jesus was *revealed* to the disciples after he was raised from the dead." By wrapping his story up with the same idea, John is helping us to see the other miracle. This story is mainly about this other miracle, and secondarily about the miracle of the

119

large catch of fish.

So what is this other miracle? The other miracle is the real appearance of Jesus after his death. "But I thought he already did that miracle?" you ask. "Didn't Jesus already appear to Mary, the disciples, and Thomas?" Yes, Jesus did appear already to Mary, the disciples, and Thomas. But each time, it was a miracle. This is no exception in John 21 when Jesus appears on the shore. This, too, was a miracle. Each time that Jesus was revealed after death, a miracle took place. Why? There are three reasons. It helps to think of these reasons temporally.

First, each time Jesus appeared, it was a demonstration of his past victory over death. Remember, it is still not normal for a person to walk and talk after death. Death still ought to have the last word. Each time Jesus appears, we are to see the miracle of his victory. Each time Jesus is revealed, we see that someone stood up to the ancient bully named death and won. When we forget how spectacular and life changing his resurrection is, we cease to see the miracle.

Second, each time Jesus appeared, it was a reminder of his present power. If the Resurrection were only a miracle the first time with his appearance to Mary, then only Mary would benefit from it. Only Mary would receive the power that is unleashed from the stand, if it is only a miracle the first time. But if the resurrection appearance is a miracle every time, then power is released every time. Then the disciples will receive power, Thomas will receive power, and seven fishermen will receive power. A miracle contains intrinsic power. Each time Jesus makes his miraculous stand we receive power. This power helps us in our present time of need.

Third, each time Jesus appeared, our future hope was brought into the present. That is a miracle greater than time-travel. When Jesus is revealed, he brings the future into the present. Jesus is our future. He represents how this world will be when the rest of creation, including you and me, is made whole. He is not broken anymore; his wounds have been healed. He comes to us from a time when there is no more brokenness or tears or pain. He is the first fruit of our complete salvation, letting us know how the rest of God's crop will turn out. Jesus comes to us as our future hope, letting us know that life stands at the end of it all. Having that solid hope right now is a miracle, for most of the time we do not foresee much good.

If we miss this miracle, we rob ourselves of victory and power and hope. It is a miracle to have a real victory when you are defeated. It is a miracle to have power when you feel so powerless in your trial. It is a miracle to have hope when you foresee nothing but failure. This means that every time Jesus stands up in your trial, a miracle occurs. You receive victory, power, and hope. The resurrection is not a doctrine that keeps to itself. When it is revealed, it is more like acid that spreads or gasses that explode. It leaves an impact on the world around it. In other words, the Resurrection is not just something for Jesus to enjoy; it is for all of creation to benefit from. It is a miracle that changes everything in its path. We must not miss this miracle.

On the one hand, John does not want us to miss the miracle. On the other hand, John conceals the miracle within everyday life, such that it has to be "revealed." This is intentional. John wants us to feel the grittiness of it all. He wants us to experience the drama of the night. We fear that they might go hungry and see that they are defeated. We wonder how their emotions are doing after all of the recent disappointments because we can relate to their struggle. This struggle could be my struggle and it could be yours. The miracle crouches in everyday life.

Why did not the disciples recognize Jesus? After all, this was the second time that he had revealed himself to them. The answer is that the Resurrection continues to be a miracle that hides itself within our lives. We do not always recognize it because it takes on different forms in different situations. The Resurrection has different implications on the shore of Lake Tiberias than it did in a home in Jerusalem. It is both the same miracle and a new miracle, all at once. It is new in that there are new implications and new battles to win. This is good news. The Resurrection adapts to us. It helps us right where we are and has fresh power for any circumstance we find ourselves in. It is not used up. It can minister to your specific situation. Like Jesus before Thomas, it accommodates to our needs and us. Each time is a revelation of goodness. We must not forget that. Each time we come to the risen Jesus, he has something good for us. Our needs do not exhaust his supply. The miracle is that he has fresh treasure for every impoverished situation.

Notice also the sensory language of the story. John mentions all of the senses: touch, taste, smell, sight, and sound. We see Jesus, feel the warm fire, taste the fish, smell the charcoal, and hear Jesus' voice. We see Peter putting on his garments, feel the water, taste the bread, smell the sea, and hear the sound of fishermen groaning to pull the net ashore. We see the night sky, feel the hunger pains, hear the waves against the boat, smell the fish, and taste the breakfast. There are more sensory stimuli that could be added. The point of loading up this passage with so much sensation is to show us that the miracle happens within real life. The Resurrection is never to be disconnected from real life—from sight, sound, taste, touch, and smell. The Resurrection is to be buried within a sea of sensation. Jesus stands in real life. The Resurrection is not an academic pet, to be stroked mainly by those in ivory towers with time on their hands. The Resurrection belongs to the people, to their daily lives, and to their endless struggles. Jesus does not watch the game from a sealed-off box office. Jesus gets in the rain and mud and plays the game with us. Jesus stands with us.

Do not miss the miracle of his stand. Jesus can stand up in your situation. Jesus is not afraid of getting dirty. Though most of us clean ourselves up to attend church, Jesus gets himself dirty when He comes to us. He takes off his royal robes and clothes himself with humanity. He is decorated with scars. He shows up anytime we need him, even first thing in the morning. He knows which lake you are fishing at. He knows that you have been up all night. So he puts himself on your shore, within your problem. The Resurrection seeks out our misery. The Resurrection is drawn to failure.

Remember, hope needs a struggle. Hope needs real life. Hope needs a real life situation to overcome. The presence of suffering does not mean that hope is gone; the presence of suffering means that hope can stand. The resurrection only happens on the landscape of hurt. Without death, there would be no resurrection. Without pain, there would be no hope. This means that with great pain is great hope. Hope is ready to stand in any situation you find yourself.

Do Not Live As If Nothing Has Happened

The disciples left the eye of the authorities in Jerusalem and headed to the middle of nowhere in Galilee. Peter said, "I am going fishing" (John 21:3). While we cannot be completely sure of their motives, it seems like the disciples are living as if nothing had happened. The last we saw them, they were locked in the home, once again, despite the fact that Jesus commissioned them by the power of the Holy Spirit to spread the news of his Resurrection. By going to a remote area, away from the throngs of people in Jerusalem, it seems as if the disciples continue to dodge their commission. John also mentions that it is night. Night is a time of ignorance and betrayal. It seems like the disciples continue to live as if nothing happened.

What is the result? "That night they caught nothing" (21:3). All of our labors are fruitless without Jesus. The disci-

123

ples can do nothing without him. They cannot even provide a few meals for themselves. Remember, the resurrection changes everything. It affects every area of our lives, no matter how small. We will never be the same if we know that one person is always standing up for us.

I imagine my wedding day. The pastor leads my wife and me in the recital of our vows and exchange of rings. He pronounces us husband and wife. We kiss at just the right time. Hundreds of people witness the ceremony and what happened that day. Then let's suppose that the next day I start to live as a bachelor. I do not pick up after myself. I eat on my own. I sleep on my own. I take care of my own finances, drive separately, and even go out with friends apart from my new wife. I do not provide for her, talk to her, or consider her opinions. I do not let her in on my life. For all intensive purposes, I am living like nothing ever happened on my wedding day. Soon I move away from home, find a girlfriend, and start a new life away from my wife. Nonetheless, I still send her an anniversary card once a year.

While this is awful to think about, it betrays how most of us live with the Resurrection. We celebrate it once a year—an "Easter" anniversary, rather than a wedding anniversary. Then we forget about it the rest of the year. We live as if Jesus never stood up after death. We live as if we do not have hope, do not have power, and do not have victory.

We catch nothing all night. We think that we are failures. We get angry and depressed and lose hope. We forget that we have a future, victory, and power. We fail to see Jesus standing on the shore while we struggle to make ends meet. We live like he is not there, does not care, and is not aware.

The Second Miracle

"Just as day was breaking, Jesus *stood* on the shore" (John 21:4, italics mine). If they will not go to Jesus, Jesus will come to them. Jesus is like light in our darkness, breaking through

124

when we are at our worst, driving away our failure. Tenderly he calls us "children" (John 21:5) and guides us to what we are looking for (John 21:6). Just as a father must provide for his children, so does Jesus need to provide for us.

So they cast it, and now they were not able to haul it in, because of the quantity of fish. *~ John 21:6*

Though they had been casting the net all night, only under the influence of the Resurrected Jesus, did they find success.

Again, it is no coincidence that Saint John uses the word "stand" in 21:4 as he did with Jesus' appearances in chapter 20. After failure and death, Jesus stood up. Here He stands up in the middle of the disciple's night of failure. He gives to them more than they could get on their own. It is clear that their catch was way beyond what is typical. This means that Jesus gives to us what we could never earn on our own. A catch this big would surely tear the nets, but "the net was not torn" (John 21:11). Being in the presence of the risen Jesus is to be in the presence of miracles.

We come to Jesus with our failures and he gives us success. Actually, it is more dramatic than that: Jesus comes to us in our failures and He gives us the success that we do not deserve. This is a life-transforming way of thinking about your failures. Your failures do not keep you from having real success. For your success does not come from you only, but from Jesus as well. Success is a fruit of the Resurrection. Success flows to us from the one standing on the shore. When Jesus stands up after death, he sends us his success. Instead of choking on the same bad apples of our toil, he gives us his own luscious fruit on which to feast.

You may think you are a failure, but you are not. You are a success. Why? Because your success does not come from you only, but from Jesus as well. When Jesus won, he won for all of his followers. His followers gain his victory; they even feel his victory. George Herbert writes in his poem Easter Wings:

> **With thee**
> **Let me combine,**
> **and feel this day thy victory**[1]

We feel the victory of the Resurrection as the weight of 153 fish in an unbroken net. Just like the first man Adam gave us his sin to feel, Jesus gave us his victory to feel. Adam kills, but Jesus makes alive (Romans 5:15-21). Adam gives us failure, but Jesus gives us victory. God gives us victory by grace and not by our works. No matter how hard we fish for success, we can do nothing apart from Jesus. Then in the presence of our failure, He gives us a net full of victory. This is the second miracle.

You Will Not Fail

But the second miracle is not random. It has a purpose and points the way for the disciples' guaranteed success. At the end of each of the four stories about Jesus, known as the four gospels in the Bible (Matthew, Mark, Luke, and John), Jesus gives His disciples a task that they will not fail. With the power of the Holy Spirit and the authority of his name, Jesus commissions his people to herald the message that will mend the broken world. God wants to save the world both spiritually and physically. The followers of Jesus are God's hands and feet, voice and heart; at work in the world. Since God will succeed, the disciples will succeed. They will succeed at catching all kinds of people for God.

That is what the second miracle is all about. Such a large catch of fish in an un-torn net points to the disciples' original mission. Jesus called the disciples to be "fishers of people"

[1] George Herbert, *George Herbert: The Complete English Works*, ed. Ann Pasternack Slater (New York: Alfred A. Knopf, 1995), 40-41.

(Mark 1:17). Early on, Jesus told His disciples that their job was to bring all kinds of people into a relationship with God. Jesus did not want a small catch, but a large catch. Jesus did not want just certain kinds of fish, but all kinds of fish. God wants a large net full of all kinds of people.

This must have seemed impossible to the disciples, who recognized the obvious barriers between people: economic, racial, religious, social, gender, and so forth. The disciples were used to God working with only a certain "chosen few." But now God was throwing the doors wide open. "How are we going to get all kinds of people?" they must have wondered. "Romans, Jews, Greeks; slaves, rulers, priests; high class, low class, no class; lepers, traitors, cripples, fornicators; drunks, punks, and monks!" All people. All kinds. Surely such a mission would tear religion in half! There is no religious net that could hold such a mass and variety of people.

God's vision is to get all kinds of people for himself. That is the voyage he is embarking on. That is the commission, therefore, of those on board with him. Together, God and his followers are going to fish for people. It is a task at which we will not fail. Our nets will be full, on the one hand, and they will not break, on the other. Apart from Jesus, we will struggle all night; with Jesus, we will succeed.

Jesus introduces us to the one task that we will not fail: telling all kinds of people about his life, death, and Resurrection. This is how we fish for people. We let people know that Jesus lived, died, and stands for them. That is our commission, of which we will not fail. You can be at sea or on the land and you will succeed. No matter how good or how bad your life feels, you will succeed at telling people about Jesus.

I love how the book of Acts ends. Acts, which is found in the Bible, narrates how God's word spreads from Jerusalem to the ends of the earth. The book ends with Saint Paul, sitting chained to a Roman guard, living without freedom. While there are many things that Paul cannot do, because of his circumstances, there is one thing that he can do. Paul can still teach people about Jesus. So the book ends with the word "unhindered." Though everything else in Paul's life was hindered. God's word was unhindered. Paul found success in spreading God's word. He did not fail at that.

> *[Paul was] proclaiming the kingdom of God and teaching about the Lord Jesus Christ with all boldness and without hindrance. ~ Acts 28:31*

Many of us suffer from low self-esteem. There may be multiple reasons why this is true. Those who suffer from low self-esteem have a keen awareness of their own failure. We know that we have messed-up. We feel our failure perhaps more than others. We beat ourselves up. We loathe mistakes, for they comment on more than our ability; they comment on our worth. We may even shy away from tasks that seem too difficult, for fear of failure. We really do not want to face our own self-esteem.

Jesus gives us a task to do, which we will not fail. Christians call this task "evangelism." Evangelism is telling all kinds of people about Jesus' life, death, and stand. Evangelism is giving hope to the hopeless. Evangelism is sharing good news with those who desperately need it. God's people will not fail at evangelism. If Jesus tells us to fish from the right side of the boat, then we will find a large catch of fish!

God's word is unstoppable, making the story of the stand unstoppable. It is pounding through the darkness. It is tearing down all strongholds. It is bringing life into deserts and fruit into famine. When God's word goes out from God, it will not return without accomplishing what God wants (Isaiah 55:11). God's word will not fail.

We must latch onto that which will not fail. That will lift

up our self-esteem. You will be amazed at how you will find success at evangelism. You may not see the effect immediately, but that does not mean that you have failed. When you plant a seed, it takes months or even years to see any results. The seed, just like the word, is at work. It will grow according to God's purposes.

Imagine a locomotive train—not much can stop a locomotive train. Think of yourself as a ribbon. On its own, the ribbon is quite vulnerable. But tied to a locomotive, the ribbon is unstoppable. The word of God is the unstoppable train that we need to tie ourselves to.

Your Story Is Special

These were fishermen; that was their story. That is where the resurrection took place, within the story of fishing. Jesus stood up within their story and made them fishers of people. Jesus did not use another metaphor. Jesus used their lives. Jesus did not introduce a whole new program. He used the story right in front of him. There are other ways of motivating disciples to evangelize. But Jesus wanted to make it personal. He wanted to make it fundamental.

Jesus validated the life of the average disciple. Recall that in John 20, he commissioned them to go out by the power of the Holy Spirit and offer forgiveness of sin. That was probably quite intimidating. In response, the disciples went fishing—they did what they knew. So Jesus follows them into their lives. He does not call them out of their story, but he stands up within their story. "You are a fisherman? Good! I will make you fishers of men!" Jesus validates their lives. "Your story is fine just how it is. I can use you just how you are. I can even use your failures at being you."

Only Jesus could do that. They were failing at being themselves, being fishermen. Jesus stands up on their shore and helps them to succeed at being themselves. This means that God wants to use our story. God wants to perfect our story. God does not want us to live out someone else's story. God has written our story so far. He does not want to erase what he has written. Rather, he wants to finish writing what he started. Just when we think we are at the last sentence, God says, "I've got more!" Just when we think the chapter should end with "zero," God writes "153."

God makes you possible. "Be yourself!" we hear. "But who am I?" I do not want to be a failure. What if I don't live up to the expectations? What if I am not accepted? I would rather put on a mask and be someone who I am not, than be myself and face rejection. We tend to think that we are mistakes. We wonder if there is any point to our existence. Jesus validates our existence. He makes it possible for me to be me and succeed. He brings to fruition the longings of our identity—to be ourselves, to be free, and to be accepted. We do not want to hide.

This also means that your story is important for the advancement of Jesus' story. God blends the two together. He turns your story into a vehicle for the declaration of Jesus' story. Then your story catches people by the power of Jesus' story. He does not just stand for himself, but he stands for you. Your story stands up when he stands up. He breathes life into dead ends and success into failure. What you thought was a plot headed nowhere, he turns into foreshadowing and anticipation of something greater. With God there are no lost or worthless bits. He leaves nothing lying back in the tomb in Jerusalem, save his grave clothes. He brings out every part of you and puts you to work in Galilee. For your story is special. There is no one like you. Your story is like a net, which God wants to fill with fish.

You thought that it was impossible for you to be you and still find success. Jesus introduces us to the God of the impossible.

The God of the Impossible

In his poem *Jerusalem 3*, William Blake writes,

I am the Resurrection and the Life
I die and pass the limits of possibility.[2]

There is so much in this verse to consider.

Do you ever find yourself saying these sorts of things? There is no possible way for me to go on right now. I see only limits. I see only walls. My net comes up empty again and again. I have failed so much that I am beginning to wonder if I am a failure. That tag will be with me my whole life: failure. Grief is my only possibility right now. I am in a dark hallway with rooms of opportunity on every side. But all the doors are shut. I sit alone. I know that life and joy are happening inside of those doors. I sit quietly in my place of failure. This is my possibility. There are no more hallways, no entrances, no exits. I am trapped by the limits of my failure.

Both Adam and Satan put their limits on us. The first person, Adam, limits us by the proclivities we inherited from him. We inherited a nature that falls into sin and evil. Though we know the right thing to do, we do the wrong thing. Sin overpowers us and brings us to our knees before it. Satan also puts limits on us. Satan tempts us and tests us. Satan seeks to ruin us. If we show signs of

life, joy, health, and spirituality, he will crush us. Adam and Satan are powerful on their own, to be sure. But when Adam and Satan scheme, a dangerous synergy erupts. What was devastating on its own, becomes lethal when combined with the other. The sum is greater than the parts. The synergy of Adam and Satan builds high walls around us, holding us back and torturing our stay.

---

[2] William Blake, *The Complete Poetry and Prose of William Blake*, David V. Erdman (New York: Anchor Books, 1988), 213.

Our whole lives we are told what is and what is not possible for us, given our education, race, socioeconomic status, experience, gender, failures and successes. Our whole lives we are told what we cannot do, because of our genetic disposition or political savvy. "Given your situation, this is possible and this is possible, but this and this are not possible." We have heard that over and over again. As we gaze into these broken mirrors, we see only lines and limits. We see only the impossibilities rather than the possibilities. We mainly avoid failing rather than striving to succeed. We genuinely expect that life will not work out for us. Adam and Satan will see to that. So our limits become just as much a part of our identity as anything else. "I am someone who cannot do such-and-such." Who am I? "I am not a good fisherman. I am not a good disciple. I am not a good friend."

How can we escape from these limits? The old Latin saying is quite true: non-posse non-peccare. "It is not possible not to sin." How can we not fail, with so much against us? To cease to fail would be to cease to be human. How is that possible?

There is only one way out. There is only one way to escape from the limits that life places on us. You have to step out of life. I have to be careful here. I do not want you to think that you, yourself have to step out of life. For you cannot step out of life and return. Only one person was able to do this. Only Jesus Christ was able to step out of life and then return to life. Let us return to what Blake wrote. "I am the Resurrection and the Life/I die and pass the limits of possibility." In order to get past all of the limits that life places on us, Jesus died. He died to all the limits and to all of the impossibilities. Knowing personally all the limits in your life, Jesus got angry. He was furious at the impossibilities that continue to drag you to your knees and keep you from the love of God. He mourned over the sins that kept you subjected as a master does a slave. There was only one way to get past these limits in your life. Jesus exited life and went down into death. While dead, he passed right by our limits. He left the influence of Adam and Satan.

Then Jesus merged back into life. Now that He has died and passed our limits, He stands on our shore; ready to give us the world he procured for us. He died and passed the limits of possibility. He brought to us the world of impossibility. In this new world of impossibility, dead people walk. In this new world of impossibility, you can catch 153 large fish without your net tearing. In this new world of impossibility, you can succeed in the morning though you fail all night. You can be fed even when your net is empty. You are found even when you are running. You are loved even when you are lost. Even though you want to sit, quit, or die, you can live. Jesus stood up with new possibilities in His wings.

The Resurrection is about bringing a new world into the old world. The old world of limited possibilities is invaded by the new world of limitless impossibilities. That may seem ridiculous to you, as it might have to the disciples. After all, why should they listen to a distant man standing on the shore, who tells them to cast out of the right side of the boat? Like they have not been casting out of both sides of the boat all night! Who did this man think he was? Why should we listen to him? Why would there suddenly be fish in a spot where a moment ago there were none? Welcome to the God of the ridiculous and impossible. When we are at our wits end, he comes and states the obvious to us. And he fills what once was empty, if we only listen to his voice. It is not about which side of the boat you cast from; it is about listening to Jesus when he stands up in your life.

That will make all the difference in the world. That will introduce you to a new world altogether. Instead of coming up empty, you will be filled. Instead of bowing to all of the limits, you will overcome. You do not have to give in or give up. There is another way. You can listen to Jesus and let him fill you up.

You remember that awful sight of Jesus on the cross. It was so hideous that even grown men hid their faces. You remember the rods, nails, spear, and beam that beat every last ounce of life from his body. Just when you remember all of this, you say to yourself, "How in the world is this man standing right now?" Then you realize that if he can stand, then all limits are off. You can stand, too.

Tear Down the Walls

I was speaking once at a conference in New Jersey. The theme of the night was "Tear Down the Walls." I spoke about the Resurrection. I shared about Mary, the disciples, and Thomas. I talked about their walls. They were trapped behind the walls of sorrow, fear, and doubt, as I described in the previous chapters. In anticipation of my message, the conference leaders built two huge brick walls. At the end of my message, people were invited to the front to write on the walls. Using markers, sticky notes, and paint, all sorts of graffiti was written on the walls. I told people to identify the walls in their lives. What were they struggling with? What was a wall in their lives? Many things were written on the walls: depression, eating disorders, substance abuse, rejection, cutting, failure, fear, insecurity, divorce, expectations, debt, and so forth. By the end, there were hundreds of "walls" written on the walls. Then I handed out hammers. I told them that it was time to tear down the walls.

The walls that looked like brick were really made out of wood. They were composed of "fake" brick paneling. So it was really quite easy to tear them down with the hammers. It was an awesome sight to see so many people pounding away at the walls in their lives, tearing right through their own limits.

Here is my point. That which looks like brick is actually

134

wood paneling. We think that the limits are formidable, unchangeable, and permanent. But they are not. They are actually ¼ inch pressed wood. While it can be hard to tear down wood, it is not impossible. With the proper tool, you can tear apart your limits limb-by-limb, brick by brick, panel by panel.

As I write these words, I notice a piece of that New Jersey wall sitting on my bookshelf. It has a single word on it: "insecurity." I am not sure who wrote that, but after the event, that is the piece I wanted to take home. I put it on my shelf as a reminder that insecurity is only made out of wood. It can be torn down.

When Jesus passed the limits of possibility and stood up, he tore down the brick walls. We need to know that. The walls that we see in our lives right now are not made out of brick, but out of wood. Satan loves to build wooden walls in our lives that look like brick. But they are not brick! You can tear those walls down and you may not even realize it. The Resurrection power you receive from Jesus can make it possible.

African Impalas

It was February of 2009. I was sitting in a conference center in San Diego, listening to Efrem Smith speak to a large group of pastors. At the end of his message, he told the story of African Impalas. Though I was sitting in a crowd of thousands, it was as if he were speaking directly to me.

The African Impala is an amazing animal. It is about the size of a dog, standing less than three feet tall. Though it is rather small, it can jump nine feet vertically and 30 feet horizontally. Given these astounding jumping abilities, one may wonder how such an animal is contained in a zoo. Efrem pointed out that in a zoo, a three-foot-high fence contains African Impalas. That is all. Though the African Impala can jump nine feet high and 30 feet long, it only takes a three-foot fence to keep it from escaping. How is that possible?

If the African Impala cannot see what is on the other side of the fence, it will not jump. Though it could easily leap over a fence three times as high, it will not. Though it has the ability, it chooses to stay behind the small walls. The African Impala could be free, but it does not even realize it.

When Jesus stood up for us, he turned us into African Impalas. We have astounding abilities because of the power of the Resurrection and the Holy Spirit living inside of us. We can overcome the walls in our lives. We do not have to stay trapped by the words writ in large graffiti on our souls. Yet we live as if we have no other choice. We live as if this is always how it will be. We live within the limits, and do not see the One standing on the shore saying, "I am the Resurrection and the Life. I die and pass the limits of possibility!" When Jesus stood up after death, he tore down the walls. We are free to go. We are no longer held hostage by sin.

There will still be walls to tear down, but they are breakable. They may feel as impossible to tear down as brick, but they are like wood—penetrable. Sometimes it takes another person to stand on your shore and tell you otherwise. You may not see it, but someone else can. I do not pretend to know your situation and your sorrow. I do not know what is written on your walls. But I do know that with Jesus there is a power that is greater than any wall.

I am certain that you are not a failure, but a success. You are not doomed to stay behind those walls forever. Because Jesus stood up for you, you will stand too. Recall from the beginning of this chapter that hope needs a struggle. Your struggle is not a sign that hope is gone, but a signal for you to start pounding down your wall. Ask God to give you the power to stand—and to leap.

The eighth reason why you must not give up is that your future is not failure.

Reason #9:

Your Purpose Is Restored

When they had finished breakfast, Jesus said to Simon Peter, "Simon, son of John, do you love me more than these?" He said to him, "Yes, Lord; you know that I love you." He said to him, "Feed my lambs." He said to him a second time, "Simon, son of John, do you love me?" He said to him, "Yes, Lord; you know that I love you." He said to him, "Tend my sheep." He said to him the third time, "Simon, son of John, do you love me?" Peter was grieved because he said to him the third time, "Do you love me?" and he said to him, "Lord, you know everything; you know that I love you." Jesus said to him, "Feed my sheep. Truly, truly, I say to you, when you were young, you used to dress yourself and walk wherever you wanted, but when you are old, you will stretch out your hands, and another will dress you and carry you where you do not want to go." (This he said to show by what kind of death he was to glorify God.) And after saying this he said to him, "Follow me."
~ John 21:15-19

137

Are We Really Going Back There?

Up to this point, we have not focused on personal sin. I have written about the human condition and we have discussed pains and trials, but I have not gotten personal yet. Now I want to get personal. We must not overlook the part we play in the pain in around us. It is crucial to learn how the resurrection of Jesus impacts sin. While there are many reasons why some of us are ready to give up, some of us are ready to give up because of guilt. We cannot stand the shame of our past much longer. As we consider John 21:15-19, we will see that there is hope even in our personal failure.

You have probably had the sort of experience with your friends or family that I have had with my wife. Inevitably, I will make some mistake or do some embarrassing thing. My wife, who is full of patience and understanding, has had to learn to deal with me over the years. Quite often, she "ignores" the behavior or words while we are still in public. She will smile and sometimes even pretend like I did not do or say whatever I just did or said. And I think I am in the clear. We will spend the rest of the day as if nothing ever happened. Then just when I am about to give a sigh of relief, when we are away from the crowd and it is just the two of us, we go back. Do you know what I mean? We go back to the moment when I had messed up.

"Are we really going back there?" I often say. "I thought everything was fine now?" But I have learned that there is no personal growth so long as our past failures are ignored.

It is a fine line, nonetheless. There are unhealthy ways of "going back there." These ways are unforgiving, un-redemptive, and oppressive, adding shame to shame. You probably have experienced this. That is not what my wife does, since she loves me and cares for me. That is not what Jesus does, either. He goes back to be sure, but he does not attack, he restores.

Peter probably thought that he was in the clear. He no

138

doubt was trying to forget that night around the campfire a couple of weeks ago. He was especially hoping that Jesus would forget that night. It is too shameful to talk about. The author John has not mentioned it since. Things were going well, after all. Jesus appeared to his disciples, as we saw, in their home. Jesus did not talk about it then. Jesus made no mention of it a week later when he showed Thomas his hands and side. They just spent the morning sitting around a campfire eating fish and bread. Surely Jesus forgot—or so Peter hoped. I am sure that during breakfast, Peter had this scene racing through his mind:

> **Now the servants of the officers had made a charcoal fire, because it was cold, and they were standing and warming themselves. Peter also was with them, standing and warming himself...So they said to him, "You also are not one of his disciples, are you?" He denied it and said, "I am not."**
> ~ *John 18:18 and 25*

Peter had rejected Jesus, not just once or twice, but three times. He did not want anyone to know—not even a powerless servant—that he was a friend of Jesus. Peter had betrayed and rejected his friend when his friend needed him the most. Who knows? Perhaps if Peter had been a better friend and fought for his Lord, Jesus might have never died? Peter, who had previously made such bold statements of fidelity to Jesus, is guilty of administering a lethal rejection. Peter hoped that Jesus had forgotten.

The Dark Journey into Shame

"Peter failed to stand by his Lord."[1] To the ancients, this was an especially shameful failure. Though we today can still feel the bite of friends or family who betray, we do not value loyalty exactly the same as those in Peter's day. Peter's Bible was

[1] *Paul Beasley-Murray, The Message of the Resurrection (Downers Grove: IVP, 2000), 112.*

filled with statements like,

> *But there is a friend who sticks closer than a brother.*
> ~ *Proverbs 18:24*

> *What is desirable in a person is loyalty.*
> ~ *Proverbs 19:22 (NRSV)*

The loyal person commits to his friend no matter what happens. The loyal person stands by his friend through the trials of life. The reason for their strong loyalty-ethic was rooted in their covenant with God. The ancient Hebrews were the people of the covenant. A covenant relationship with God marked every nook and cranny of their lives. So much so that "the ultimate disgrace for a covenant people is to be disloyal (Hosea 4:1)."[2]

That is what Peter felt: ultimate disgrace. Peter did not just betray his friend or brother, Peter betrayed God himself. Peter, whose whole life was supposed to echo a covenant love for God, turned his back on his own Maker. This was the worst thing that Peter had ever done. He never wants to make the dark journey into his shame and disgrace again.

We all have these dark moments in our lives. We all have memories that haunt rather than help. We have all had moments of weakness around the fire, when we failed to stay true to our families, our friends, or ourselves. We have all traded in our morals for a few morsels (Hebrews 12:16). We have said things, done things, or believed things that we now utterly regret. We try to forget the past, but it keeps leaching into the present, like the muck through the casing of a landfill. It makes us sick. So sick, that we are depressed, self-medicated, unbearable, and defeated.

---

[2] Leland Ryken, James C. Wilhoit, and Tremper Longmann III, eds., *Dictionary of Biblical Imagery* (Downers Grove: IVP, 1998), 518.

And now Jesus wants to go back.

Jesus did not forget what happened around the campfire. It is no mistake that they now find themselves around another charcoal campfire (John 21:9). Jesus is gently bringing Peter back to that place. He does not come out with guns blazing and bring up Peter's denial. Jesus does not come with an axe, but with a surgeon's scalpel, entering our pain carefully. To make the connection clearer to Peter, who rejected Jesus three times (John 18:17, 25, and 27), Jesus asks Peter three questions. Each of these questions has to do with Peter's commitment to Jesus. "Simon, son of John, do you love me more than these?" (John 21:15). Notice that Jesus does not call him "Peter," the name that means, "rock." For Peter did not stay strong like a rock. Jesus is reminding Simon of that. "Simon, son of John, do you love me?" (John 21:16). Then he asks a third time, "Simon, son of John, do you love me?" (John 21:17). Jesus asks Peter to accept him the same amount of times that he rejected him.

Jesus is not afraid to go into your pain or to recall your shame. Jesus will go where you do not want him to go. He knows that it is eating you alive. He knows that you have no ability to deal with your past. You are trying, but it is not working. You are addicted to self-help. The irony is that you keep failing at trying to make your failures better. They simply will not go away. Our hands are raw from constant scrubbing as we try to make ourselves clean. Like Lady Macbeth, even our sleep is consumed with guilt.

> **Doctor:** *You see, her eyes are open.*
> **Gentlewoman:** *Ay, but their sense is shut.*
> **Doctor:** *What is it she does now? Look, how he rubs her hands.*
> **Gentlewoman:** *It is an accustomed action with her, to seem thus washing her hands. I have known her to continue in this a quarter of an hour.*

Lady Macbeth: *Yet here's a spot...Out, damned spot. Out, I say!—One, two—why then, 'tis time to do 't.* [3]

Jesus takes the dark journey in order to get rid of the spot on our soul. He goes back to the place that we would never go on our own, but where we all long to go, if we only had some help.

The Resurrection Makes This Journey Safe for Us

Here is the ninth reason why you must not give up: your purpose is restored. But in order to restore your purpose, Jesus must make the journey into your pain. It is going to be uncomfortable. We want to pretend like there is no need for him to do so. "If we go back there, then everything will blow up," we assume. "It will not get better, but worse." We feel that it is unsafe to travel through our pain. It was hard enough the first time, why go there again?

Do not forget, however, whom it is that makes this journey. Actually, do not forget what kind of person wants to make this journey. A person who was dead and now alive wants to make this journey—and that makes all the difference. Jesus had already been to the depths of human depravity when he hung on the cross. He had already felt the weight of every affliction known to humankind on his shoulders. He bore every explosive sin, every repulsive situation, and every terrifying sickness known to our world. He went down into the grave with the burden of it in his being, absorbing every bit of it. Then he stood up in triumph.

He had already taken the sting out of Peter's denial. He had already felt the blast of every sin of every one of his followers, exploding against his perfect soul. From the cross he cried out not only, "Father, forgive them," but also, "It is finished!" (Luke 23:34 and John 19:30, respectively). He had already

[3] William Shakespeare, *Macbeth*, ed. Burton Raffel (New Haven: Yale University Press, 2005), 142.

journeyed into every dark pit. Now he stands at the surface, ready to take us back down, only now it is safe to do so.

I do not think it is a mistake that the author John mentions three sets of threes in these verses. First, Jesus asks three questions ("Do you love me, etc"). Second, Peter gives three answers ("Yes, Lord…etc."). Third, Jesus gives three commands ("Feed my lambs, etc."). Previously, we noted that this reminds us of Peter's triple denial. Now, however, we are reminded of another "third." It was on the third day that Jesus stood up from the grave. John's three threes help us to see that it is the resurrected Jesus that we are dealing with. It is not just anyone; it is the Risen One.

Jesus is like a minesweeper, which goes ahead of us into our pain to take care of the bombs. A minesweeper is a naval ship that goes ahead of the fleet in order to detect and neutralize the mines lurking underwater. As we have learned, Jesus himself absorbs the blast of the mines. He detonates the resurrection against the mines, causing a more powerful explosion than our sin. Jesus goes ahead into the murky water and makes it safe for his fleet to pass through.

Jesus made it safe for Peter to go back through his past failure. There were going to be no more explosions this time. Lives would not be lost; Jesus had made sure of that. We fear going back into our pain because of how it condemns us. We think that it will explode again, taking even more casualties. We believe that it will give God yet another reason to despise us and punish us. Jesus knows better. Jesus made it safe for you to live with your past.

He took away all condemnation, "There is therefore now no condemnation for those who are in Christ Jesus" (Romans 8:1). He absorbed all punishment, "But He was wounded for our transgressions; He was crushed for our iniquities; upon Him was the chastisement that brought us peace, and with His stripes we are healed" (Isaiah 53:5). He bore all the pain that was headed for us, "The Lord has laid on him the iniquity of us all" and "He bore the sin of many, and makes intercession for the transgressors" (Isaiah 53:6 and 12). Friend, God does not condemn you anymore. He swept through your sin and died to make you His.

John Calvin wrote that Jesus is like our attorney in court who hides our sin in his coat, such that the judge cannot see. Instead of arguing our case with our works, he argues our case with his works. Jesus offers his perfect good works in our defense. He displays His righteousness to the court rather than our unrighteousness, which remains buried in His side. We have nothing to fear from our past. We are safe with Jesus.

For Christ's righteousness, which as it alone is perfect, alone can bear the sight of God, must appear in court on our behalf, and stand surety [as our complete deposit] in judgment, Furnished with this righteousness, we obtain continual forgiveness of sins in faith. Covered with this purity, the sordidness and uncleanness of our imperfections are not ascribed to us but are hidden as if buried that they may not come into God's judgment.[4]

Second Chance

So why do we have to go back through those waters? Jesus does not remind Peter of his past in order to shame him, but to empower him. Jesus wants to give Peter a second chance. Only now, Peter will live his life with a new power source: the standing Jesus.

My father and I replaced the engine in my car several years ago. After two days of working, we finally got the new engine in place. The old engine lay defeated on my garage floor (actually, it was resting on an old skateboard). The new engine was completely bolted, belted, and wired in my car. Then came the moment of truth, I got behind the wheel and turned the

[4] John Calvin, *Institutes of the Christian Religion: 1559 Translation Edition*, eds. McNeill and Battles (Philadelphia: Westminster John Knox Press, 1960), 82.

key. Nothing. Not even a flinch from the engine. We spent the next two hours trying to figure out what went wrong. Then in a flash of inspiration, my dad went to the old engine and took off a three-inch plate. After just minutes, he had the old plate screwed onto the new engine. Then it started right up.

The magical plate was a part of the old engine's computer system. The new engine needed the memory of the old in order to ignite. Though my car had a new engine, it needed a little piece from the past to make it run. For the computer to recognize this new engine, it needed to go through a piece of the old.

In chapter five, we learned that God loves to employ our pain. God loves to turn our suffering into service. God loves to take a piece from our past and give it a new engine.

Notice the paradox of what Jesus calls Peter to do in John 21:15-19. Jesus calls Peter to be loyal to his sheep. Jesus calls Peter to be faithful to God's people—not to walk out on them. But that is exactly the sin that Peter committed against Jesus! Though Peter rejected Jesus, Jesus calls Peter never to reject his people. Jesus brings Peter back through the pain of his failure in order to give him another chance at the same thing, only this time Peter has a new engine.

Jesus makes it clear that Peter will remain loyal to the end this time,

> ***Truly, truly, I say to you, when you were young, you used to dress yourself and walk wherever you wanted, but when you are old, you will stretch out your hands, and another will dress you and carry you where you do not want to go.*** ~ *John 21:18*

Jesus, as John explains in the next verse, is referring to Peter's execution by crucifixion. Peter will remain loyal to Jesus' sheep until death. Peter will never deny Jesus again. This is truly amazing. But it never would have happened if Jesus did not make the dark journey into Peter's pain. Jesus had to take out the old engine in order to put in a new. Nonetheless, he still needed a piece of the old.

Glory

As you can see, the Resurrection makes Peter's purpose possible. Peter's purpose was to glorify God (John 21:19). It is utterly amazing to see how Peter best glorified God. Peter best glorified God through the very thing that he most sinned against God—his loyalty. What once was his most shameful act, being disloyal to Jesus, now becomes his most sacred offering. The way that Peter best glorified God was his extreme loyalty to God, to the end, even through the terrible ending of crucifixion.

This is simply staggering: God rehabilitates our sin and turns it into glory. What you thought was your worst moment, and it was, can be made into your most glorious. What you thought was your weakest point; God turns into your most shining strength.

What you are ready to call it quits over right now, God wants to restore. God wants to turn your burden into blessing. God wants to transform your shame into glory. God loves to use sinful people to bring him glory. You are no exception. You have a purpose. You must not give up now, because God has a plan for your pain. Let Jesus go down into your pain, absorb all of its penalties, and bring you back through it with a new engine. There is so much in store for you, if you will only let Jesus in. You are on the verge of a miracle. God's purpose for your weakness is his glory.

Starting with Weakness

Mark experienced this. Mark grew up with Tourette's syndrome. This syndrome caused Mark to lose control of his bodily urges. It caused him to curse repeatedly. He would bark out obscenities at home and at school and everywhere in between. It was so embarrassing for him. Neither could he control the urges of his arms, hands, and legs. He would twitch and turn in spastic response to wild impulses beneath his skin. Tourette's left him with little but a broken soul at the end of most days. He felt friendless and unwanted. He felt like a freak. He cursed God and cursed himself; he thought that there was no hope.

Then Mark told me that God came into his life. God took control of him; and Mark gave his urges to God. "God, you take my urges to curse violently." Then God did. Though Mark had cursed hundreds if not thousands of times each day, God gave him power over the urges. Soon Mark began to live "normally." Though the internal rush of Tourette's still raged within, he was able to control the appearance of it. Mark progressed so much that it seemed the Syndrome had left.

Then, in yet another great irony of God, Mark went to graduate school and became a pastor. Today, Mark is a minister. God took his foul mouth and filled it with grace. What once had been Mark's curse was transformed into his greatest way of giving glory to God. Now his mouth offers blessing to those around him rather than cursing.

If God can use the Apostle Peter's disloyalty and Mark's cursing, then he can also use you. What is the thing that breaks you beyond repair? Could it be that God wants to use that for his glory? That stain in your life that you feel is farthest from God is actually God's starting point. Jesus loves to start with our weaknesses.

What we thought was the end of us, God wants to use as a beginning.

Light of the World
One day Jesus took a hard look at his followers (Matthew

147

4:24-25 and 5:1). Every one of them was a sinner. There were drunkards, prostitutes, gluttons, and the greedy. They were broken and diseased and demon possessed. They ached, they had epilepsy, and some were paralyzed. They broke the law, did not know the law, and did not care about the law in the first place. They were not the religious type, in fact, the religious type made every effort to keep them hidden. But not Jesus.

In a stunning declaration, he stood before his followers and said,

> ***You are the light of the world. A city set on a hill cannot be hidden. Nor do people light a lamp and put it under a basket, but on a stand, and it gives light to all in the house.***
> ~ *Matthew 5:14-15*

Jesus did not wait to tell his followers that they were the light of the world. He could have waited until they were healed and whole. He could have waited until they were a bit more sanctified and holy. He could have waited until they died and went to heaven, saying something cliché like, "One day when you pass from this earth you will become a star in heaven, giving light to those struggling on earth." But Jesus did not say that. He said shocking things, not safe things.

Jesus looked at the crowd of inglorious sinners and said, "You are the light of the world," right here and right now. They did not have to wait any longer to shine like stars and give glory to their Father in Heaven. They could get up on the stand now, tragedies and all.

Think about the kinds of things you put on display in your home. You put the best things on display. You put artwork, family pictures, and trophies on display. You put that which is precious to you on display, that which you are proud of. On the other hand, we hide the things that we are ashamed of. We hide the things that we do not want to be displayed for all to see. We hide the things that we are not proud of. When guests come over to our homes, we fill our closets with all the junk we do not want others to see lying around.

Jesus looks at the crowd and says, "I am proud of you!"

Jesus wants to put you on display, just how you are. You are his artwork, his family picture, his trophy. He wants to put you on display for all to see. Yes, you! You are precious to him and he is not ashamed of you. He does not want to stuff you in the closet or hide you under a basket. He wants to get you out and put you on display on his stand. You are the light of the world.

You may want to go under the basket, as Matthew 5:15 describes. But you do not belong under a basket. You belong on the stand so that you can give glory to God. Here is how Jesus' declaration ends,

> *In the same way, let your light shine before others, so that they may see your good works and give glory to your Father who is in heaven.* ~ *Matthew 5:16*

Your Purpose

So what is your purpose? You were made to give glory to God. How do you best do that? Let us go back to John 21:15-19 to find out. Academics have gotten so sidetracked with the precise meaning of Jesus' statements to Peter about caring for his sheep. Jesus uses' different verbs and nouns in his commands, creating all sorts of confusion. But if we focus on this, we miss where it all is going. Whatever Jesus means by "caring for the sheep," it is all going to glory. Peter is to love God by loving others in such a way, that he dies in the process. As I said, he was called to be loyal to the end.

> *This he said to show by what kind of death he was to glorify God.* ~ *John 21:19*

149

But even this is not the point of the passage. Jesus summarizes the whole thing, mysterious triple statements and all, with just two words: "Follow me" (John 21:19). That is the point. That is how we fulfill our purpose and glorify God the most.

To follow Jesus is to mimic his life. Just as Jesus cared for his followers, so was Peter called to care for his followers. Just as Jesus stretched out his hands and died on a cross, so was Peter to stretch out his hands and die on a cross. Just as Jesus' death was the ultimate display of God's glory (John 12:27 and 28), so will Peter's death be the ultimate display of God's glory. To follow Jesus is to follow the pattern of his life, to live for what he lived for and to die for what he died for.

Jesus restored Peter so that Peter could follow him. That was Peter's purpose.

That is your purpose. I know what it feels like to think that you have no purpose in life. I know what it is like to want to give up. I have been on the edge before, not able to see the point of it all. In these moments, we need to hear the firm command of Jesus: "Follow me." By following Jesus, we will be lead to places where our weaknesses can be used for God's glory. We will be used by God to restore others, just like us. Or, as Jesus said, "Feed my lambs…tend my sheep…feed my sheep" (John 21:15, 16, and 17).

Pulling Trees

As you stretch yourself out to follow Jesus, it might feel like he has you between the trees. Let me explain with another car story.

One of my dad's hobbies—actually, it was his only hobby—was restoring wrecked cars. Throughout my years growing up, I have literally seen hundreds of wrecked cars in our garage. These cars were not just a "little" wrecked, either. These were classified as "totaled." When my dad went to the auction to get a car, he let the nice ones go by. He did not want to bring home the shiny, new cars. Instead, he had his eye on the cars that nobody else wanted. He would bid on the wrecks, the cars that seemed hopeless.

The flatbed truck would bring these cars to our home. I would experience the same wonder each time, "How in the world are we going to get this one straightened out!" To me, it looked impossible, but to my dad, "all cars were possible" (cf. Matthew 19:26!). After all, if left up to me, the cars would never get fixed; but if put into the hands of the mechanic, there is hope.

So many of our themes are merging at this point: the auction, passing the limits of possibility, and hope for the hopeless. I imagine myself as a wrecked car on which God has his special eye. He gave his Son on the auction block so that he could take me home. Entrusted into the hands of the Master Mechanic, there is hope for my restoration.

I need to tell you about how my dad restored the worst of the worst cars. These cars not only had mangled bumpers, hoods, and quarter panels, but also their frames were bent and buckled. I have seen every type of wreck possible, rear-end collisions, side-impacts, front-end collisions, rollovers—even cars smashed by telephone poles, which fell on the roof. The cars that had crooked frames were the ones that had to go between the trees.

There were four trees in my backyard that my siblings and I called "the pulling trees." They roughly made the shape of a huge rectangle. My dad would push, drag, or pull the totaled car and put it in the middle of the pulling trees. He would chain each corner of the car to one of the four trees. Then he would hook-up a come-along-winch to the chains. He would begin to crank the winch. I can still hear the sound of the cranking to this day.

Soon the chains would become taught. The cranking would become more difficult and slower. The chains would become so tight that one could walk on them. Then it started to happen. The car would start to bend back into shape. The tension was enormous; there would be the sound of cracking and popping from the car. You could hear the metal straining as the chain put huge amounts of pressure on it. The frame of the car would unfold slowly to where my dad wanted it to be. For us kids, it was a terrifying experience, we always had to "stand back!" We were always silent as the mechanic went about the business of straightening the crooked.

When you thought that the car could not bear one more crank from the winch, when you thought it all would fly apart if any more tension were put on those chains, my dad would slowly crank it one more time. He would always over-adjust the frame, just to make sure the car would not bend back toward its wrecked shape when the chains were gone.

Satisfied, he would look at the whole project and say five words. He would say the same five words each time. We always knew these words were coming. Sometimes we would try to say them before he did. Nodding his head at the car, which was under incredibly intense pressure from the chains, he would say, "Now it has to soak." Those were the five words. The car had to "soak" in that position for a while. If he let the chains off right away, the metal would flex back into its wrecked position. The car had to soak in the position that the mechanic wanted it in order to effect permanent change.

The mechanic did not go easy on the car if he wanted to restore it.

Sometimes we feel like God has us between the pulling trees. We are chained at every side of our lives and the tension is incredible. The effect is painful. All we hear is cranking and bending and popping. It feels like we are going to fly apart. God gets us just where he wants us—the shape that is perfect for us—and then he lets us soak.

As you read these words, some of you are soaking right now. You feel the chains on your life. You are not sure what is happening, it is confusing and agonizing. Having been picked up from the auction you thought life was going to get better, not worse. But here you are between the pulling trees, in God's hands, and life could not seem to get any worse. You are soaking in it.

Truly, truly, I say to you, when you were young, you used to dress yourself and walk wherever you wanted, but when you are old, you will stretch out your hands, and another will dress you and carry you where you do not want to go. ~ *John 21:18*

In order to be restored to your purpose, you need to go where you do not want to go. You do not want to go between the trees, but God wants to restore you there. You want to live for yourself and take your life into your own hands. But God wants you to live for others and put your life into his hands. This is how you glorify God with your life and fulfill your purpose.

Prisoner of Hope

This book is not called, "Ten Ways to Have a Pain Free Life." God does not call us to a pain free life. He calls us to find hope in the pain. So far we have discovered nine reasons why we must not give up. The ninth reason is that your purpose is restored. We have seen that restoration is painful. Nonetheless, there is no hope without pain. You will never discover hope apart from first finding pain.

Our world is "totaled," but God is restoring it. He is putting it back into shape. God loves to turn our weaknesses into strengths. There is hope for your personal failures. Even more, God is giving each of his followers a purpose. When Jesus

153

stood up after death, he gave you a purpose. He wants you to follow him. He wants you to bind yourself to him.

Jurgen Moltmann lived through the horrors of WWII. He was a prisoner of war in a camp after the war ended. Though he went on to become a world-renowned scholar, he never forgot the lessons he learned as a prisoner. By reading a Bible that a chaplain gave to him, he discovered hope in his prison.

> *I knew with certainty: [Jesus] is someone who understands you. I began to understand the assailed Christ because I felt that he understood me: this was the divine brother in distress, who takes the prisoners with him on his way to resurrection. I began to summon up the courage to live again, seized by a great hope.*[5]

If anyone understands what it is like to be between the trees, it is Jesus. He was stretched out long before Peter would be stretched out. Since Jesus went to the chains first, he understands us. Now he comes to us as a brother in our distress. He takes us prisoner with him on his way out of the grave. As he stands, he binds us to himself so that we can stand with him. We become a prisoner of hope. I pray that you would summon up the courage to live again because you know that you will stand in the end.

[5] Jurgen Moltmann, *The Source of Life: The Holy Spirit and the Theology of Life*, trans., Margaret Kohl (Minneapolis: Augsburg Fortress, 1997), 5.

Reason #10:

You Are Essential

Peter turned and saw the disciple whom Jesus loved following them, the one who had been reclining at table close to him and had said, "Lord, who is it that is going to betray you?" When Peter saw him, he said to Jesus, "Lord, what about this man?" Jesus said to him, "If it is my will that he remain until I come, what is that to you? You follow me!" So the saying spread abroad among the brothers that this disciple was not to die; yet Jesus did not say to him that he was not to die, but, "If it is my will that he remain until I come, what is that to you?" This is the disciple who is bearing witness about these things, and who has written these things, and we know that his testimony is true.   Now there are also many other things that Jesus did. Were every one of them to be written, I suppose that the world itself could not contain the books that would be written.
~ John 21:20-25

More Glorious

Jesus is more glorious than we could ever imagine. What Saint John says is no hyperbole.

Now there are also many other things that Jesus did. Were every one of them to be written, I suppose that the world itself could not contain the books that would be written. *~ John 21:25*

Just as John began his book with the glory of Jesus, he also ends his book with the glory of Jesus. At the beginning of his book, John explains how Jesus was the "Word" who created the world. The Word has always existed as God. It stands to reason that if the Word created the world, then the Word is greater than the world. If the Word is greater than the world, then the world would not be able to contain the Word. What John says is quite true. The glories of the Word exhaust the resources of the world.

Jesus is greater than you think. John leaves his story of Jesus open-ended. He leaves us both craving to know more and straining to comprehend. We simply cannot imagine the worldwide library that he describes. If every centimeter of this world were filled with ancient scrolls, even then there would not be enough papyrus to record the doings of Jesus. You would need another world, which is staggering to envision. You may even need ten worlds. Jesus is greater than you think.

What would these books be about? They would be about the mighty doings of Jesus in our lives. They would be stories of the stand, from ancient times until now. Remember, the resurrection means that he still stands; and if he still stands, then he still works, from times long ago until this very moment. Thus, the library would be about him and us at the same time. Page after page, we would marvel at his work in our lives. We would read stories of rescue and redemption. There would be stories of healing and provision. There would be millions more resurrection encounters in these pages. The resurrection has so much power and potential that John cannot even describe it all in one place. John just shared a few stories, but there are so many more. Jesus is greater than you think.

The Other Half

But there is more. Here is the part that we did not expect. It is not just that Jesus is great; that is only half of the story. Jesus is more glorious than you think—and so are you.

You are greater than you think. We forget this in so much of our thinking. There are two things that we have to know: God is great and so are we. We get our glory from him. He supplies our glory. The stories that the world cannot contain are about his work in our lives. This means that we are a part of his story. We are in his collection of books, which overflow from this world to the next.

To use another analogy, because Christ is a glorious mosaic, you are an essential piece. Henri Nouwen writes,

Community is like a large mosaic. Each little piece seems so insignificant. One piece is bright red, another cold blue or dull green, another warm purple, another sharp yellow, another shining gold. Some look precious, others ordinary. Some look valuable, others worthless. Some look gaudy, others delicate. As individual stones, we can do little with them except compare them and judge their beauty and value. When, however, all these little stones are brought together in one big mosaic portraying the face of Christ, who would ever question the importance of any one of them? If one of them, even the least spectacular one, is missing, the face is incomplete. Together in the one mosaic, each little stone is indispensable and makes a unique contribution to the glory of God. That's community, a fellowship of little people who together make God visible in the world.[1]

[1] Henri Nouwen, Can You Drink the Cup (Notre Dame: Ave Marie Press, 1996), 58.

You are essential. You may feel insignificant on your own, but you are not. You may be dull or sharp or shining. But you are essential. We need you to take your place next to the other stones in the mosaic. Together, we make the face of Christ. Without you, the face is incomplete. You are indispensable to the whole project. God's glory would not be the same without you. Seen this way, how could you ever question your importance? You are a glorious stone in the glorious face of Christ.

Words Become Flesh

The beginning of John's book not only mentions the Word (John 1:1-3), but also it mentions witness,

There was a man sent from God, whose name was John [the Baptist]. He came as a witness, to bear witness about the light, that all might believe through him. He was not the light, but came to bear witness about the light. ~ *John 1:6-8*

Now recall our passage in John 21, which mentions all the words that could be written about Jesus (verse 25) and the witness of John the Apostle,

This is the disciple who is bearing witness about these things, and who has written these things, and we know that his testimony [witness] is true. ~ *John 21:24*

Both passages contain the ideas of witness and word. But here is a third connection between the beginning and end of John's book. John 1 goes on to say,

The Word became flesh and dwelt among us. ~ *John 1:14*

The pattern in both the beginning and the end of John's book is as follows: Word, witness, and flesh. "But," you ask, "Where is 'flesh' mentioned at the end? We clearly see the reference to words about Jesus. We also see the idea of witness in John 21:24. But where does John tell us that the 'Word became flesh' in John 21?"

That is why John does not complete his story. That is why he leaves the reader on edge. He leaves it open-ended. "The world itself could not contain the books that would be written." That is how John ends his story. In this verse, we are to see the "en-fleshment" or incarnation once again. The incarnation is the next, unwritten verse. John wants the reader to see himself as the continuation of the story.

You are the rest of the story. You en-flesh the word of God within this world. Just as the Word of God became flesh and dwelt among us, we also give skin to the gospel and dwell within this world. We give flesh to the word. We continue the story about Jesus. We are the new place where God dwells, the living and breathing temple of God, the stones that make up the mosaic of Christ. "You yourselves like living stones are being built up as a spiritual house, to be a holy priesthood" (1 Peter 2:5).

That is why we are essential. We carry the story and priesthood of Jesus forward. We are "John 22," the next un-written chapter.

It is not that John did not want to fill the world with stories about Jesus. He wanted to, but he could not do that. There is just too much to say. God is saying what he wants to say through those who follow Jesus Christ, then and now. You complete the face of Jesus in this world. Without you, the picture would not be whole.

What You Show Me

You show me something about Jesus that I would never have known without you. The way he has worked in your life is spectacular. The new things he wants to do in your life are glorious. You will soon be the recipient of new grace, outpoured on your life in abundance. Do not call it quits before that. We need you. You are essential. It would not be the same without you.

On the one hand, God's glory is his alone and he is perfectly sufficient and glorious without humans. Scholars call this God's aseity. God does not need anyone other than himself. I affirm God's glory. Nonetheless, on the other hand, our glorious God decided to make creatures for his glory (Isaiah 43:7). By making us, his glory shines even more. Now the world sees a side of God that would never have been emitted, were we not made. The cosmos would never know what unconditional love is, were it not for you. There is nothing more beautiful than the sight of unmerited love. There is nothing more glorious than the restoration of a sinner into God's family. There is nothing more moving than a prodigal who comes home. Angels rejoice over you. God's glory increases because of you. As you grow in brilliance, so does God. That is why you are essential. Bury yourself in God's glory. Let it be your shield, comfort, and sword. Battle doubts with it. Protect your mind with it. Soothe your soul with it. Because of God's glory, there is a place for you to shine in this world and the next. You are not just essential, you are more glorious than you ever imagined.

Piles of Colored Powder

Let me tell you about the best "thank-you" card that I have ever received. It was brilliantly colored. There were three piles of powder on the front, each a warm hue of red or orange. On the back of the card was written, "Piles of colored powder used for worship in India." The person who gave me the card scribbled these words on the inside, "You add color to our church." As I said, that was my favorite card. So much of the time, even as a pastor, I am unsure of myself. I envy others who have better gifts. I do not feel like I have the right personality or experiences.

But this friend said that my "color" was a blessing. God made me to shine for him in a specific way. God made you to shine for him in a specific way, too. Both of us were created for his glory. You may have moments of shame. You may feel inadequate. You may despise certain features of your life. But God sees us all as his piles of colored powder and he uses us for worship. God uses you for his glory. He uses your size, your strengths, and your personality. He uses your abilities and in-abilities. God loves your face, your quirks, your hobbies, and your desires. He knows your trials and temptations. He lives through your experiences. He stood by you in your past and will be there in the future. He can use every part of you for his glory. That which you do not like about you, God likes about you. He has a plan for it. He can use it. He spends it all in worship.

Peter Turned

Then Peter took his eyes off of Jesus.

So much good had been happening. Jesus had rescued Mary from sorrow, the disciples from fear, and Thomas from doubt. Jesus turned the disciples' failure into success and restored Peter's purpose. Despite all the good, danger still lurked. For just a moment—and it only takes a split second—Peter took his eyes off of Jesus and compared himself to another,

> ***Peter turned and saw the disciple whom Jesus loved following them...and said to Jesus, "Lord, what about this man?"***
> *~ John 21:20 and 21*

161

Peter took his eyes off of the big picture, the glorious face of Christ, and compared one small stone with another. Peter thought that one stone might be more fortunate than another. He thought that one stone might be more essential than another. He allowed envy into his heart.

Envy

Just when you start to see that there is a lot of good happening in your life, your eye catches another. Just when you start to feel good about yourself, you notice the fortunes of someone else. Suddenly, you are back to where you began, wrestling with hopelessness.

Unlike sorrow, fear, doubt, or failure, envy does not feed off of trials. It feeds off of fortune. That is what makes it so devious and subtle. Envy is underhanded. It launches its attack indirectly. That is why you are in danger of envy now, rather than before. Envy does not live in the trenches, when we are struggling to find just one more reason to go on. Envy stalks after the dust settles and the sun begins to shine. It starts as a gentle rain. But it quickly rushes and turns into a torrent. Soon it sweeps us away and we go right back into the trench. Face down in the pit; we wonder if there is any good in our lives.

Envy can do this in the blink of an eye, when you least expect it.

In the last chapter, we learned about Peter's fate. Peter would be faithful to Jesus to the end. In fact, Peter would be crucified for his faith. Before that, Peter would persevere through pastoral ministry, taking care of God's flock. His life would be difficult and ultimately cut short. We are given the impression that it would be a bitter struggle, such that Peter would constantly have to depend on his love for Jesus if he was going to make it. After all, Jesus asks him three times, "Do you love me?"

Rumors were spreading about another apostle, John. It was rumored that John would not have such a bitter life. In fact, it was rumored that John would live forever. After just hearing about his most horrific fate, Peter cannot resist comparing himself to John. No doubt Peter was envious. So he took the opportunity to ask Jesus about the rumors,

Lord, what about this man? ~ _John 21:21_

Peter compares himself to John. Both are disciples. Both were among the closest friends of Jesus. Both had made immense sacrifices to follow Jesus. Both were fishermen. But, for some reason, one was going to enjoy long life and the other was going to die by execution.

Consider the following thoughts about envy from Aristotle,

It is also clear on what occasions people feel envious and of whom, and what condition they are in, if envy is a certain pain at the prosperity of those like oneself in regard to the good things mentioned, not in order to get anything for oneself but just because they have it. The sort of people who will feel envy are the ones for whom there are, or appear to be, others like themselves, and by "like" I mean race, family, age, traits of character, reputation, and possessions.[2]

First, we will note, according to Aristotle, that envy happens among those who are similar to each other. This was the case with Peter and John. Envy is the strongest when we hold the most things in common: age, gender, socioeconomic status, race, education, resources, experiences, character traits, etc. Given that two people are so similar, why did fortune fall on one person and not the other? This facilitates the question we

[2] _Aristotle, Plato Gorgias and Aristotle, ed. Joe Sachs (MA: Focus Publishing/R. Pullins Co., 2008), 212._

ask ourselves, "Why wasn't that me?" Why did John receive a long life and Peter crucifixion? Counting all things as even, this fortune could have happened to one just as easy as the other.

Second, we will note that the truly envious person does not necessarily desire the fortune itself, but the worth that comes with it. The envious person desires the fortune, in this case, long life, not in order to get long life, "but just because they have it." I do not want the thing itself, but I want the sense of worth that comes from knowing that I got it and you didn't. Put negatively, I cannot stand the thought that you got it and I didn't. Surely you are not more worthy than I am?

Envy causes us to lose sight of our intrinsic, God-given worth. Since the other person received the fortune, we assume that he was more worthy to receive it in the first place. By having our eyes fixed on his fortune, we somehow feel that we are worthless. That is why we are envious. We want to regain the sense of worth that comes from having fortunes. We do not want the fortunes themselves, but the worth that goes along with them. Thus, we are parasites, living off of secondhand worth. We fail to remember that we have God-given worth. We fail to feast on the worth that God has given to us as those who bear his image. Envy keeps me from being human. Humans have intrinsic value and worth. Envy tells me that value is found elsewhere, not in our humanity, but in our fortunes.

No wonder people kill for love and possessions. They are really killing for an identity. They are fighting for the right to exist. Worth is relegated to achievement. "And if I do not achieve, then I'm not worth keeping around."

Unhappiness

"Next to worry, probably one of the most potent causes of unhappiness is envy."[3] The biblical book of Proverbs says similarly,

[3] Bertrand Russell, *The Conquest of Happiness* (New York: Horace Liveright, 1958), 67.

A tranquil heart gives life to the flesh, but envy makes the bones rot. ~ *Proverbs 14:30*

Why does envy rot the bones? Why is envy one of the most potent causes of unhappiness? First, envy causes us to be dissatisfied with God's will. We do not like the way that God has set our boundaries. We do not like the fact that we are tall or short, American or African. We wish we were born into some other family or into some other situation. To envy the situation of another is to be dissatisfied with what God has allowed in your life.

Second, we are dissatisfied with ourselves. We have low self-esteem. We do not think we have much worth. We lose sight of our intrinsic value. We no longer see ourselves as created in God's image. We long for another image—the image of the person we envy. Their image becomes our idol, our god. Too much envy leads to sorrow. The envious person will eventually turn into the depressed person. After all, we feel like we are not worth keeping around.

Third, envy causes us to be dissatisfied with the other people. When I envy you, I cease to care about you. My eyes are not on you, but on your good fortune. I may even grow to despise you. I will feel like you do not deserve the fortune. I will try to find your faults. I will draw attention to my strengths and to your weaknesses. This is how envy turns into aggression. We fight over who is better. It is my perceived value against yours. We get defensive when our weaknesses are pointed out. We are suspicious of the motives of others. We paint ourselves into a corner and cannot escape. The only way out is to fight.

Being dissatisfied with God, ourselves, and others; our bones begin to rot. We are not happy. Everyone is an enemy. Everyone is out to get us. We cannot enjoy life or the gifts that

God has given us.

Consider Jesus' parable of the vineyard workers (Matthew 21:1-15). A master of a house hires laborers for his vineyard. Before he hires them, he tells each one that they will receive a denarius (the amount of a day's wage). He goes out at about every other hour to hire workers. He promises the same wage to each worker. When he finally paid the workers at the end of the day, some were upset about the wage of one denarius. "And on receiving it they grumbled at the master of the house, saying, 'These last worked only one hour, and you have made them equal to us who have borne the burden of the day and the scorching heat'" (Matthew 20:12). They were not satisfied with the fortune of those who worked less, but received the same wage. They felt that the master of the house should have been more gracious with those who worked longer. In fact, they thought that the master was not being fair for not being more generous. The master of the house replies,

> *Friend, I am doing you no wrong. Did you not agree with me for a denarius? Take what belongs to you and go. I choose to give to this last worker as I give to you. Am I not allowed to do what I choose with what belongs to me? Or do you begrudge my generosity?* ~ Matthew 20:13-15

The master paid everyone in the end. However, he was more generous with some than with others. But they all received what they agreed upon. The workers who were angry forgot that the master is allowed to give however he wants. If he wants to give generously, then what is that to us? Or, as Jesus said in John 21:21, "If it is my will that he remain until I come, what is that to you?" Jesus, like the master of the vineyard, can give as he pleases. Who are we to argue? Some will get what they deserve and others will get what they do not deserve. Grace is a gift that we do not deserve. Envy wants to give people what they deserve and refuses to see grace. Envy does not focus on the Master, but on the fortune. Jesus wants us to get our eyes off of the material and put them on the Master. God gives some people what they deserve and he gives others more than they deserve; but he can do with his grace whatever he wants.

Peter needs to put his eyes on the Master. He needs to see that Jesus can do with his grace whatever he wants. If he wants John to live longer, then that is his prerogative. Peter is not called to follow either John or himself—his own desires. Peter is called to follow Jesus.

Jealousy Fights Envy

Jesus looks deeply into Peter's envious eyes and says, "You follow me!" There is no way around what Jesus is saying. Peter's eyes were straying. Peter was going off course. He was following after fortune. He was giving his heart away to something else.

That is when Jesus gets jealous. It is important to understand the difference between envy and jealousy. Envy just involves two people, yourself and the other. Jealousy involves at least three people, you and the other, plus a threat. Envy puts up walls between two people. Jealousy builds a wall around two people so that a third cannot get in. Envy destroys relationships. Jealousy guards relationships. Envy has its eyes on a fortune. Jealousy has its eyes on love. Envy fights against another. Jealousy fights for another.

Here is how envy and jealousy exist in John's story. Peter envied John. Peter had his eyes on John's fortune, not John. Peter turned his back on John. Relationships were crumbling between Peter and John and between Peter and Jesus. That is what envy does. It rots. On the other hand, Jesus was jealous for Peter. Peter was going after another "love." Peter was more interested in long life than he was in being in a relationship with Jesus. Jesus was not going to put up with that. Notice that Jesus did not even answer Peter's question. Jesus went on the offensive. "What is that to you?" he said. "You follow me!" he demanded. Jesus was jealous for Peter. Jesus did not want Peter to follow after other things. Jesus wanted Peter to follow him.

God is jealous for you. He wants you all to himself. Unlike human jealousy, God's jealousy is pure and not destructive. God always has our best interests in mind. That said, God's jealous love guards us from giving our hearts to things that will hurt us. He does not want you to give your heart away to cruel masters. He does not want anything to keep you from following him. He does not want your eyes to stray. He does not want to see you lusting after other things. He wants your heart all for himself and he will give you all his heart in return. He is jealous for his people. He wants a one-to-one relationship. That is why the first Commandment is "You shall have no other gods except me" (Exodus 20:3). Jealousy seeks to build a wall around a relationship in order to protect it from outside threats.

Seen this way, jealousy overcomes envy. That is how Jesus deals with Peter. Though Peter takes his eyes off of Jesus, Jesus does not take his eyes off of Peter. Jesus tells Peter, "Get your eyes on me. You follow me!" Were it not for Jesus' jealousy, envy would have rotted the bones of Peter. Peter would have kept his eyes off of Jesus and on other things. There is no health or happiness when your eyes are not on Jesus. Jesus is our health.

Until I Come

Finally, notice the small phrase tucked within Jesus' words to Peter: until I come. Jesus wants Peter to follow him until he returns. I do not mean to overstate the obvious, but this means that Jesus stays alive. "Until I come" preserves hope. Jesus is alive and he will return. Jesus still stands, in other words. He will stand the whole time you are following him. He will keep being jealous for you. He will fight for you. He will not sit down on you. He will not quit on you, though you feel like quitting on yourself.

"Until I come" gets my eyes off of the things I envy. Instead, I look to Jesus. I long for his return. I look to the day when he will return for his bride, the church. Then everyone will have life and fortune. We will experience love like never before. We will receive our great treasure, which we have been storing up during this life. By focusing on Jesus' return, I refuse to let envy rot my life. I refuse to let it have control of me. There is health in anticipation of the Lord's coming. That is why "waiting on the Lord" is a source of strength.

But they who wait for the Lord shall renew their strength; they shall mount up with wings like eagles; they shall run and not be weary; they shall walk and not faint. - Isaiah 40:31

Waiting on the Lord gives hope; it does not take hope. Envy, on the other hand, takes hope away.

Do Not Let Go

Jesus had a plan for Peter. Jesus had a plan for John. Both of these men were essential. Jesus has a plan for you. He is jealous for you and will fight for you. He calls you to latch onto him.

Annie Dillard writes a personal essay called Living Like Weasels.[4] Consider these paragraphs from the beginning and ending of her work.

"Once a man shot an eagle out of the sky. He examined the

---

[4] Annie Dillard, Annie Dillard Reader (New York: Harper Collins, 1994), 123 and 126.

eagle and found the dry skull of a weasel fixed by the jaws to his throat. The supposition is that the eagle had pounced on the weasel and the weasel swiveled and bit as instinct taught him, tooth to neck, and nearly won. I would like to have seen that eagle from the air a few weeks or months before he was shot: was the whole weasel still attached to his feathered throat, a fur pendant? Or did the eagle eat what he could reach, gutting the living weasel with his talons before his breast, bending his beak, cleaning the beautiful airborne bones?...

We could, you know. We can live any way we want. People take vows of poverty, chastity, and obedience—even of silence—by choice. The thing is to stalk your calling in a certain skilled and supple way, to locate the most tender and live spot and plug into that pulse. This is yielding, not fighting. A weasel doesn't "attack" anything; a weasel lives as he's meant to, yielding at every moment to the perfect freedom of single necessity.

I think it would be well, and proper, and obedient, and pure, to grasp your one necessity and not let it go, to dangle from it limp wherever it takes you. Then even death, where you're going no matter how you live, cannot you part. Seize [the eagle] and let it seize you up aloft even, till your eyes burn out and drop; let your musky flesh fall off in shreds, and let your very bones unhinge and scatter, loosened over fields, over fields and woods, lightly, thoughtless, from any height at all, from as high as eagles."

Latch on to that which latches on to you. When God swoops down and grabs hold of you with his talons, turn to him and latch onto him. Open your jaw wide and bite down hard on his neck. Do not let him go. Hold on to him with all you have, like Jacob did when he wrestled with his God (Genesis 32:25-26). Or, as Jesus said to Peter, "You follow me!" God is your "one necessity."

Then you will soar. You will leave the ordinary dirt you were used to living in. You will rise up with wings as eagles. You will achieve new heights. You will be no ordinary weasel. Imagine, if the other weasels could speak, what they might say when you fly past, "Look at that weasel! Look at her go! Look at him soar! That is no ordinary weasel!"

Hold onto Jesus with all you have. When Jesus stood up after death, he did not rise up empty handed. He grabbed a hold of you with his talons. As he rose, so will you rise. Grab hold of that which is grabbing hold of you. Feel the force of the Resurrection taking you to new heights. The resurrection grabs us when we are low, not when we are high. It is something that happens to us, not something we have to produce from within ourselves. It is not subjective hope, but objective power. In the end you may be stretched out like Peter. Or in the end you might write a book like John. No matter. Let God take you wherever he wants to take you, until "your very bones unhinge and scatter."

Conclusion:

Alien Hope

Hope stands outside of you. It does not come from within you. You will not always find hope if you search for it within your own being. Hope comes from the outside, as a person walking to you in a garden or standing on the shore, calling your name. Hope is not found in your actions, but in the actions of another, on your behalf. Hope is not found in your achievements, but in the achievements of another for you.

Martin Luther was fond of referring to the goodness that comes to us from Jesus as "alien righteousness" because it comes to us from the outside. It "is the righteousness of another, instilled from without."[1] We have no righteousness or goodness of our own, so we must depend on the righteousness of another. Jesus gives us his righteousness. We make it our own, though it was alien to us. It came from the outside.

It has been the purpose of this book to demonstrate to you that we have an alien hope, standing outside of us. It comes to us from another source and we can make it our own. It is a free gift from God. It is light in our darkness. Hope is an event, not an emotion. It is not contingent on the conditions of your life. Hope stands no matter the condition. It is unconditional and alien hope.

[1] Martin Luther, *Martin Luther: Selections from His Writings*, ed., John Dillenberger (New York: Anchor Books, 1962), 86.

173

Right now, you have ten solid reasons why you must not give up. These are not subjective. They are not faddish. They are not based on human systems or wisdom. They are not ten steps for you to find hope. They are ten reasons to prove that hope has already found you. Since God himself did this for you, these reasons will stand no matter what, even when you feel like falling.

> *Hope does not put us to shame, because God's love has been poured into our hearts through the Holy Spirit who has been given to us.* ~ Romans 5:5

When your spirit is crushed, when your eyes turn down because of shame, and when you are empty to the point of being overwhelmed, God wants to pour out his love on you. When you are an empty container, he will fill you. When you are hiding, he will find you. When you fall, he will stand.

Trials Turn into Thrones

What do you see when you look at your trial? I know that seems like a ridiculous question, on the level with someone who asks if it hurt when you accidently touched your hand to the stove. When you look at your trial, hopefully you see a trial. But if we allow our eyes to see from God's vantage, we'll see more.

Consider two places in Scripture where God give us double-vision. First, in Revelation 5, the Apostle John looks at Jesus in heaven. Jesus appears as both a lion and a lamb. Lambs, of course, represent sacrifice or trials. Lions, on the other hand, represent ruling and victory. The ancients used to place statues of lions on both sides of their royal thrones, to demonstrate their king's power to rule and dominate. When John looked for sacrifice, he also saw victory. Is it a Lamb or a Lion, a sacrifice or a victory, a cross or a throne?

174

The next Scripture is Hebrews 12:2. "Let us fix our eyes on Jesus, the author and perfecter of our faith, who for the joy set before him endured the cross, scorning its shame, and sat down at the right hand of the throne of God." The context of this verse is that of encouragement for weary Christians; the writer seeks to motivate Christians to persevere when life gets heavy and hard, instead of giving up. To support his point, the writer gives the ultimate example, that of Jesus on the cross. Jesus had to endure the ridiculous cruelty of being hung on a cross, left exposed to mockery and plunged into mortality.

Then in the same breath, we find Jesus sitting down "at the right hand of the throne of God." At one moment, he was in the lowest ranking position that humans could design, the cross; in the next, he is sitting at the highest ranking position the cosmos could offer, the throne. When we look at Jesus' great trial, we end up seeing his great victory.

What do you see when you look at your trial? If you think that it all ends in blood, then you've missed it. Trials turn into thrones. Life is headed to victory.

When Jesus stands up after his death, he stands up on the rubble. The Resurrection happens at a cemetery, not a party. When God chooses to unleash a victory, the backdrop he selects looks more like pain than power. Jesus' stand ushers victory into our lives.

The thing that you're ready to call it quits over is the place where God wants to start building his throne. God loves to start with lambs and crosses and weakness. Because of this, I have learned to hear the sound of the soldiers pounding the nails through Jesus' hands differently. It's not just the sound of hammering defeat, it is also the sound of building a throne for victory.

There are ten reasons why you must not give up. At every moment of your life, hope stands in victory.

Acknowledgements

There are several people that I would like to thank for helping me with this project. I owe a huge thanks to Tim Anderson and Tim Traver for their encouragement and endless work on the Hope Stands website. What great memories we have! Thanks to Steve Hiller for putting together an excellent promotional video. Thanks to Fred Von Kamecke and Katie McCoach for helping me with my sentence structure and for your helpful insights on the chapters. Thanks to Jackie Larson for combing through and catching several mistakes in my early drafts (any that are left are mine!). A special thanks to Tremper Longman for giving me helpful feedback and guidance. I am also very grateful to Colin Smith for his friendship and support. I would like to acknowledge a fantastic group of students who stand behind me at North Suburban Church. Thank you for your prayers and enthusiasm for Hope Stands. I would like to thank everyone at Ellechor Publishing House, especially those I worked the closest with, Rochelle Carter, Alvetta Rolle, and Caroll Atkins. Finally, and most importantly, I owe a huge thanks to my wife, Shantè, whose endless care and prayers keep me going.

Appendix:

Did Jesus Rise from the Grave?
Seven Pieces of Evidence

1. Jesus really died.
   a. The blood and water give proof (John 19:34).
   b. Professional Roman executioners oversaw the crucifixion (Luke 23:47).
   c. Jesus did not just pass out. There was too much trauma done to his body (Matthew 27:26-31).

2. The place of Jesus' burial was known.
   a. The tomb belonged to a well-known and upstanding person, Joseph of Arimathea (Luke 23:50).
   b. The Romans put a seal on the exact place where Jesus was buried (Matthew 27:66).

3. The tomb was empty.
   a. The guards could not find the body, even though their lives depended on it.
   b. Jesus' enemies presuppose the tomb is empty, because they give excuses as to why the body is not there (Matthew 28:12-15).
   If the body were there, they could just point to it and stop all the excitement. But there is no body to point to.

4. The body was not stolen.
  a. The Jewish authorities would not have stolen it. That's what they were trying to prevent!
  b. Grave robbers wouldn't have stolen it, because they left behind the grave wrappings, the most valuable thing there!
  c. The disciples would not be able to steal it, because of in ability, fear, and the Roman guard.

5. They knew exactly which tomb to go to.
  a. Multiple eyewitnesses watched where Jesus was put in the tomb and would not forget the location in only 72 hours (Nicodemus, Joseph, and the women).
  b. Since the guards' lives depended on the tomb being secured, it was very unlikely that they were guarding the wrong tomb. So they knew where it was for when the authorities would question them in search of the body.
  c. The chief priests would not have offered a large sum of money to bribe the guards if it were just the case of a mixed-up tomb (Matthew 28:12).
  d. Anyone in the city who knew the tomb's owner could easily have pointed out the correct location of the tomb to dispel all doubt.

6. There were many resurrection sightings.
  a. Matthew 28, Mark 16, Luke 24, John 20-21.
  b. Acts 1, 9, 10, 18, 23, and 26.
  c. Revelation.
  d. 1Corinthians 15:3-9. This passage mentions more than 500 eyewitnesses! Ancient historians used first hand eye witnesses for writing works of history. They did not use second or third-hand sources, but first hand witnesses. Each witness would be known by local readers and could be called upon at any time to give an account for their claim (either proving or disproving the claim).

7. The account is not a legend or myth

    a. A legend is a story that lacks accurate historical evidence. In contrast, the gospels are full of proper names, dates, cultural details, historical events, and customs.

    b. A myth is a fictitious story or unfounded belief about a person with no real existence. There is more evidence for Jesus' exitence than any other ancient figure. The written accounts date from about 5 years after the Resurrection, which is not enough time for a myth or legend to develop. All of the eyewitnesses were still alive and could easily dismiss a claim were it not true.

For further reading on the resurrection, see William Lane Craig's The Son Rises: The Historical Evidence for the Resurrection of Jesus (Eugene, OR: Wipf and Stock Publishers, 2001).